MW00682334

ERRAND BOY
IN THE
MOOSELAND
HILLS

J. MAGNUS BJARNASON

TRANSLATED BY
BORGA JAKOBSON

Formac Publishing Company Limited
Halifax, Nova Scotia

Copyright © 2001 by Formac Publishing Company Limited

All rights reserved. No part of this book may be reproduced or transmitted in any form or by any means, electronic or mechanical, including photocopying, or by any information storage or retrieval system, without permission in writing from the publisher.

Cover Illustration: [untitled], E. Thresher 1820s (Courtesy: NSARM)

Formac Publishing Company Limited acknowledges the support of the cultural affairs section, Nova Scotia Department of Tourism and Culture. We acknowledge the financial support of the Government of Canada through the Book Publishing Industry Development Program (BPIDP) for our publishing activities. We acknowledge the support of the Canada Council for the Arts for our publishing program.

National Library of Canadian Cataloguing in Publication Data

Bjarnason, Jóhann Magnús, 1865-1945
[Vornætur á Elgsheiðum. English]
    Errand Boy in the Mooseland Hills

Translation of: Vornætur á Elgsheðum
ISBN 0-88780-541-8

1. Bjarnason, Jóhann Magnús, 1865-1945. 2. Mooseland (N.S.)—Anecdotes.
3. Authors, Canadian (Icelandic)—Biography. 4. Icelandic Canadians—
Biography. I. Title

PS8501.J37Z5313 2001	C839.683	C2001-903034-7
PT7511.J5287Z4713 2001		

Formac Publishing Company Limited
5502 Atlantic Street
Halifax, Nova Scotia B3H 1G4
www.formac.ca

Printed and bound in Canada

CONTENTS

Dedication   5
Acknowledgements   6
Introduction   7
Cousin Ármann   21
Mabel McIsaac   37
Eyvindur   47
Sighvatur   57
Bessi   69
Boy Burns   81
Abraham Burt   93
Patrick O'More   105
Hákon Farmann   117
Bergljót   133
Hafliði   143
The Pedlar   153
An Old Sea Wolf   165
The Icelandic Sherlock Holmes   173

These translations are dedicated in memory of my parents
Kristjon Sigurdson,
who was a pupil of J. Magnús Bjarnason
and
Indiana Sveinsdóttir Sigurdson,
who was herself an Icelandic immigrant

ACKNOWLEDGEMENTS

I thank my children for their interest in this project. I especially thank Bill Perlmutter for helpful advice and Kristine Perlmutter for typing and preparation of the manuscript.

I am grateful to the Icelandic Memorial Society of Nova Scotia for its interest in the work of Jóhann Magnús Bjarnason and for these translations, in particular. I am especially grateful to its secretary, J. Marshall Burgess, Q.C., for a great deal of background information with regard to the history of Nova Scotia around the time of the Icelandic settlements. Nelson Gerrard of Eyrarbakki Icelandic Heritage Centre at Hnausa, Manitoba, was also very helpful to this project.

INTRODUCTION

Jóhann Magnús Bjarnason was born on May 24, 1866, on a farm called Meðalnes í Fellum in eastern Iceland. The farm was located in Jökuldal (Glacier Valley), near the river Lagarfljót. His parents were Bjarni Andrésson and Kristbjörg Magnúsdóttir. In Iceland, surnames are rarely used. Typically, Icelandic names include a given, or Christian name and a patronymic, which consists of the father's name and an ending ("son" for a male child or "dóttir" for a daughter). Jóhann Magnús was usually called Magnús and further identified as Bjarnason because he was the son of Bjarni, According to Icelandic custom, he is called Magnús in this introduction.

As a young child, he enjoyed the long summer days that Iceland is famous for. He also enjoyed the closeness of many relatives. As was the custom in Iceland, he was taught to read and write at home. During long winter evenings he listened to the older folk retell sagas or recite poetry while they worked at spinning, knitting or other handicrafts. Thus began a love of stories that he carried with him throughout his life.

Economic conditions had long demanded a frugal lifestyle among the Icelandic people; some looked across the ocean and wondered about opportunities in a new land. A few had followed Mormon missionaries to Utah; a small group had emigrated from Iceland to Brazil. After the American Civil War, Icelandic people began to move to the United States. At that time, advertisements appeared offering free land in Canada to interested settlers.

In 1875, a huge volcanic eruption occurred in central Iceland and ash caused widespread damage to farms and flocks. Many farmers saw only one option; their only hope lay in relocation and settlement on the west side of the Atlantic. It was hard for emigrants to know where they should go. Some left for Wisconsin and Minnesota; others left for Ontario and Manitoba. A few went directly to Nova Scotia. Among those were the families of Bjarni Andrésson, Magnús's father, and Guðbrandur Erlendsson. Before the end of 1875, some twenty-five Icelandic families had come together in a settlement that had been planned for them in an area known as Mooseland Hills in Halifax County.

Little did the n ew settlers know that successive waves of immigrants had arrived in Nova Scotia during the past century. Acadians had been returning after their expulsion in 1755; German Lutherans and other Protestant groups had settled in Lunenburg County. Large numbers of Loyalists had moved to Nova Scotia after the American Revolution. Hundreds of people arrived from overpopulated areas of England and Scotland, and there were many Irish immigrants. Most of the good agricultural land had been claimed by the time the Icelanders arrived. In view of all this immigration it is surprising that the Province was offering inducements to new settlers.

After Confederation, John A. Macdonald's government

put emphasis on the building of the railways, settlement of the interior and immigration. Several federal-provincial conferences on immigration were held in Ottawa. At first, the government of Nova Scotia took a negative approach but, according to the throne speech of 1870, William Annand's government gave serious attention to it. Did they have to meet some commitment to the federal government? Did they feel that they could comply with the federal government's agenda, offer a home to needy immigrants and at the same time, meet local demands? These questions might be intriguing, but perhaps the answers don't matter. The stories in this book make no reference to politics; they simply tell an immigrant boy's experiences, which illuminate quite succinctly the historical accounts.

In order to provide a little background about the Icelandic settlement in the Mooseland Hills, it is helpful to recall some developments that had taken place in the area during the 1860s. In 1858, gold was discovered in the area; by 1869, mines were in operation at Moose River, Caribou and Tangier. A road through the district was needed in order to develop these mining centres. A settlement in the area seemed like a logical solution to the situation. Settlers could provide needed supplies for the miners; mining towns would be a market for any surplus farm produce. Furthermore, the Mooseland Hills area was Crown land, one of the few areas left at the government's disposal.

At the beginning of May 1875, plans had been made for establishing an Icelandic community in Mooseland Hills; some of the settlers had already arrived. Premier Annand suddenly resigned from the government and left to take a position in London, England. Philip Cartaret Hill now had to take responsibility for implementing the plans for the settlement.

The original scheme was to build the road from Musquodoboit to Mooseland, a distance of twenty-six kilometres. The Icelandic men would be paid one dollar per day, and they would work with a gang of local men under a foreman. The government offered one-hundred-acre lots with one acre cleared to each man over fifteen years of age. A log house would be built for each family. Basic provisions were to be supplied for one year and settlers had to clear two acres annually for the next five years. After that time, they could apply for deeds to their land.

Meanwhile, some of the families were housed in a large building in Musquodoboit that became known as Iceland House. In 1915, Guðbrandur Erlendsson wrote down his recollections from the time he spent there. "The view from Iceland House was very beautiful. I think that the main reason that we enjoyed our stay in Nova Scotia so very much was the grandeur of the countryside. Our plans for the future and our dreams of a better life gave us hope that our new homes would be beautiful. The Musquodoboit Valley is so pretty . . . . The residences, built a comfortable distance apart, have beautiful gardens most of which are surrounded by white fences . . . . To the south of the valley are hills of varying sizes . . . named Mooseland Hills. Between the hills run deep but small streams, ponds and rivers, the largest of which is the Moose River, along whose banks lie fields of hay and grassy meadows. However there is much land which is quite useless . . . . Some tracts of land are covered with heather . . . . Boulders are covered with moss and, strangely enough, huge fir trees some towering up to a hundred feet high."

The Icelandic men spent five months working on the road which was cut through heavy bush. This was an unfamiliar experience for them because there were no forests in Iceland. Guðbrandur wrote that the more he saw of the forest, the more he began to wonder about the soil. By the end of September the road was finished but plans had changed. The proposed road from Musquodoboit to Mooseland would have brought the settlers within ten kilometres of the railroad. Critics of the government managed to have that changed so that the road went instead from Musquodoboit to Tangier, a distance of forty-eight kilometres, with the result that the settlers were now sixty-four kilometres from the railroad.

While the road was being built, surveyors were commissioned to measure out thirty-six lots for the Icelanders at the headwaters of the Tangier River. The surveyors said they "took pains to select only lands fit for cultivation."

During the fall, one-acre plots were cleared on each farm and twenty-five log houses were erected. They were built of straight fir logs, notched to fit, with a floor of unplaned boards and finished with a shingled roof. The settlers moved in before the end of the year with basic provisions such as flour, syrup and tea, and plenty of fuel. It was understood that they would have to rely on hunting and fishing to complement their diet. However, the moose had been hunted almost to extinction and lumbermen had dammed the Tangier and Moose rivers. Consequently, the trout no longer swam upstream, so fishing was poor.

By the spring of 1876, a schoolhouse had been built in the middle of the settlement, and the schoolmaster, Alexander Wilson, moved into his home. The schoolhouse was also the meeting house and place of worship. The first order of business was to choose a name for the community. The unanimous choice was Markland, which is Icelandic for woodland. Markland was the name given to one of the forested lands described by Leif the Lucky in the Icelandic Sagas.

The farms were also given names, as is the custom in Iceland. Bjarni Andrésson and his wife named their home Hlíðarhús, which means "house on the hill."

Guðbrandur's farm, called Grœnavatn (Green Lake), had a grassy stream and a pond, but when he tried to plough the acres he had cleared he found rocks upon rocks. The farms varied from lot to lot; along the banks of the Moose River there was good land for growing hay.

The settlers chose their own lay minister, and his weekly worship services were well-attended, although everyone had to walk to get there, in some cases long distances. There was a remarkable community spirit, and people found comfort in helping each other. Lutheran ministers from the German congregation in Lunenburg visited the settlement and performed special duties such as baptism, confirmation and marriage ceremonies. They did all this out of kindness to fellow Lutherans and refused any payment. During these ceremonies, the ministers spoke English but they allowed the lay minister to prepare the children for confirmation by using Icelandic texts.

The schoolmaster, Mr. Wilson, was a recent arrival from Scotland. He was described as a "very learned man" and was considered an excellent teacher; his pupils progressed remarkably well. Not only did the government build the schoolhouse, but they also paid the teacher. "Not one penny did we pay in taxes during all the time we spent in Nova Scotia," wrote Guðbrandur, "which shows how eager the government was to keep us healthy and happy." The settlers were grateful for the public-school system that had been introduced into Nova Scotia during the 1860s. In Iceland children usually depended on home schooling with the occasional assistance of itinerant teachers.

Only the younger children were lucky enough to go to school; Magnús Bjarnason was one of them. It appears that he attended for the first few years and then intermittently thereafter. Mr. Wilson taught him to read, write and speak English and encouraged him to continue his education by reading English literature. This was the foundation for his appetite for reading.

Older children, like their peers in other communities, had to seek employment outside the settlement. Labour regulations in Nova Scotia mines forbade the employment of children under ten years of age, but they did allow for boys of ten to twelve years old "to do light work as long as the work-week did not exceed sixty hours." The young men from the settlement found various jobs in gold mines, lumber camps or on farms, especially at harvest time. Young girls and single women accepted positions as domestic servants. Wages were low, especially for women. However, this was a kind of education, observed Magnús in his later years, because the young people became familiar with the customs of the country, practised English and "learned many useful things."

Magnús was employed in various positions. During the period he lived in Nova Scotia, from the age of nine to sixteen, his inquisitive nature and his interest in people, combined with a keen eye to absorb and record many events and new impressions in his places of employment.

He had to do a fair amount of walking. Road conditions were abysmal. A stagecoach provided weekly mail service to Musquodoboit, but most people walked wherever they had to go. If someone passed by with a cart they usually offered rides to those who were travelling on foot. On long trips, people often had to stop at farmhouses to ask for a meal and lodging for the night. Payment would be offered, but some farmers wouldn't hear of it, saying that it would be wrong to charge overnight guests. During this time, there was rail service from Halifax to Truro, which took three hours and cost $1.83—nearly two days' wages. In the story of Hafliði, it is said that he walked from Dartmouth to Truro and back each year.

Magnús observed the Icelanders striving to make something of their farms. Clearing the land was back-breaking work, especially when the main tools were axes and hoes. "The soil was so infertile," noted Guðbrandur, "the longer we stayed the more we became aware that there was nothing ahead but poverty and want. The farmers who lived west of us were an example of what the future held, for after years of toil they were still poor." Nor were they alone. Rural areas in the province differed greatly in geographical character, from the rich farmlands in the river valleys to the rocky coasts of the Atlantic Ocean. Subsistence food production or low-paid wage-labour was the only option for many. Indeed, during the 1880s, there was a significant out-migration. Many rural people were leaving because of the lack of opportunities and because of the attraction of prosperous areas elsewhere in the country.

The settlers' growing discontent was understandable. Meanwhile, other problems were coming to light. It seems that there was a lack of understanding by the government about the expectations of settlers. The Icelanders hoped that friends and relatives would eventually join them in Nova Scotia; the government was only prepared for thirty-six families. Although they had reason to expect more immigrants in 1876, they seemed totally at a loss as to what to do for them when they arrived. Finally they bought some land near Lockeport and offered small lots to people in the hope that they could find work in the fishing industry. In the Assembly, the government was criticized for their expenditures on behalf of the Icelanders. In the end, the Province admitted that an immigration grant from the federal government that had been paid for several years had been cut off; the Province could no longer afford to take part in the immigration scheme. Premier Hill's government, which has been so generous to the first group of Icelanders, was defeated in the 1878 provincial election. When Simon Holmes came into office, immigrants were no longer invited to Nova Scotia, but a few came anyway in search of family members. The government maintained a small budget for their assistance but most immigrants were directed to Manitoba.

By 1880, the Canadian Pacific Railway was reaching the Prairies and there was a boom in Winnipeg. Wages rose to an unprecedented high of about three dollars per day. Farming conditions in Manitoba were reportedly quite good; new land was opening up in North Dakota as well. Large numbers of Icelandic people were finding homes in these areas. In 1881, the Markland settlers started collecting deeds to their farms and selling their holdings to move "out west." In some cases, buyers dismantled the houses and left the rest. Animals were auctioned off. Provisions had originally been offered as loans, but now those loans were forgiven, which was a gift in itself. After 1882, only a few Icelandic people remained in Nova Scotia; many looked back with regret. In spite of poverty, they had enjoyed the beautiful countryside, moderate weather, good health and good neighbours.

After Jóhann Magnús Bjarnason moved to Manitoba, he worked at a sawmill and at other jobs and he attended a collegiate institute in Winnipeg when he had the financial means to do so. He attended Normal School, a teachers' college. In 1887, at the age of twenty-one, he was married. That same year he published a small book of poems, thereby launching his writing career. In 1889, he began teaching, which suited him well because of his love of learning. His dedication and his innovative teaching methods earned him the respect of his pupils; they revered him because of the personal interest he took in them. The students paid visits to Magnús and his wife, Guðrún, whenever they had some time off. They were always treated well by Guðrún, and they understood when Magnús withdrew to work on his writing. Magnus's schooling in Markland and his experience in English-speaking communities proved to be a great asset. His life in Markland may have shaped his idea of community. Dr. Jóhannes Pálsson, a former pupil, wrote about Magnús during his early teaching career in Geysir, Manitoba. At that time, in 1892, there were only three or four people in the area who could speak English, and Magnús was the only one who could read and write English with any confidence. Thus it fell to him to write letters for all his neighbours, to fill out documents and assist with any legal matters, both as an interpreter and often as an unpaid legal adviser. There was never a program or a concert in Geysir to which Magnús did not contribute. He held Christmas concerts in connection with the school and set up drama clubs every winter, writing the plays, directing the performances and coaching the actors.

In his spare time he pursued his writing career. He wrote a novel, *Eiríkur Hansson*, which was published in three parts in 1899, 1902, and 1903 and takes place in Nova Scotia.

Around this time, Magnús began to suffer from ill health, no doubt related to overwork. He had to leave teaching for a while, but in total he taught for more than thirty years in the Icelandic districts of Manitoba. For his excellence in teaching, the Manitoba Educational Association appointed him an honorary member.

During his retirement years in Elfros, Saskatchewan, Magnús continued to write. His published works include books of poetry, short stories and anecdotes, three full-length novels, a children's book and many journals and newspapers articles. Unfortunately, some important pieces of his writings still remain in handwritten texts, unpublished.

On his seventieth birthday, the Parliament of Iceland conferred on Magnús its highest honour, the Order of the Falcon. He was also named Honorary Member of the Icelandic National League of North America in recognition of his work. Readers from Canada, the United States and Iceland sent words of appreciation and good wishes.

All the selections in this book were originally contributions to Icelandic journals that were published in Winnipeg in the early part of the twentieth century. Of course, these modern "sagas" are illumined by the personality of the narrator. However, I believe they are all based in fact. In the original publications final notes are often separate from the body of the work, as if for explanation or verification. Often the note adds little to the story except to make it clear that the person described was real. For example, in the story of Eyvindur in the original 1943 publication a note explains "if Eyvindur is still alive, he would be about eighty-five years old." Three of the stories were first published in *Almanak* (Ólafur S. Thorgeirsson, Winnipeg). They all have similar short notes at the end. These first stories were "Mabel McIsaac" (1906), "An Icelandic Superman" (1909), and "An Icelandic Sherlock Holmes" (1910). These three stories were republished along with "Bergljót," and "Patrick O'More" and other stories in the first edition in 1910 of *Vornætur á Elgsheiðum* (Spring Evenings in the Mooseland Hills).

The other nine stories in this selection were all gifts to the Icelandic annual publication *Tímarit* and were issued one at time over a twelve-year period, 1932-44. In the 1944 story of Sighvatur, the author begins by saying, "I remember clearly" and ends, "This is the story that Sighvatur told the Icelandic miners in August, 1880." All fourteen stories were collected and included in the second edition of *Vornætur á Elgsheiðum* which was published in 1970 in Akureyri, Iceland, twenty-five years after the author's death. The stories are written in a rambling style, almost as though Magnús was reminiscing with a group of friends. He shows no bitterness over the hardships of the pioneers but sometimes a note of wistfulness creeps in. Many stories mention early deaths. Magnús never uses the word but his readers would have understood a reference to tuberculosis, which was rampant in Iceland and many other

European countries in the 1800s.

It has been my pleasure to translate these stories from the original Icelandic text. I believe that they offer a true picture of the immigrant experience and provide a glimpse into rural life in Nova Scotia in the 1870s and 1880s.

—Borga Jakobson

COUSIN ÁRMANN

At least three Icelanders had spent some time in Nova Scotia before the Icelandic settlement at Mooseland Hills was established in 1875. One of these three was a man called Ármann. I only knew him by his first name. I want to tell his story, although I realize that he never told me very much about himself. He never visited the settlement, and few of the settlers came to know him personally. Few of them ever mentioned Ármann, and I suppose that none of them knew his family or from what part of the country he had come. He was unmarried and had come out all by himself.

I met him during the summer of 1879 in Dartmouth. I was an errand boy at the time for an older man of Scottish descent, Edgar Oswald, who lived a short distance north of the town. I was asked to help out while his son Robert was at sea. Robert Oswald was first mate on a ship that sailed between Halifax and Kingston, Jamaica.

I remember as clearly as if it had happened yesterday how I felt when I left to take this job. I was thirteen years old and this was the first time that I had left home for any length of time. A Scottish farmer had offered me the job. His name was Mark Miller and he lived only a short distance from the Icelandic settlement. My parents knew him to be a good

man. He arrived one evening in the beginning of May to take
me to Dartmouth and he spent the night with my people.
Early the next morning we started off in a two-wheeled cart
pulled by a bay horse. I was so excited about the journey that
I had hardly slept all night. The weather was sunny and
pleasant when we left the settlement and, for the most part,
the road was wide and smooth, especially after we entered
the Musquodoboit district. Mark Miller was an interesting
companion, and I greatly enjoyed hearing some of the stories
he had to tell. I was curious and I asked ever so many questions, and he answered good-naturedly. I wanted to know a
little bit about Mr. and Mrs. Oswald. He said that they were
fine people and that Mr. Oswald was a particular friend of
his. In fact, they had been friends from their boyhood days.

"You won't mind staying with those good people," Mr.
Miller repeated several times during the journey.

"Then there is an Icelander in Dartmouth," he mentioned
on one occasion, "and you can look him up and talk to him
in Icelandic."

"Have you seen him?" I asked.

"No, but I have often heard him mentioned."

"Do you know what his name is?" I asked.

"No, I don't know, but I have heard that he is an excellent
carpenter and he has his shop at Allan Archibald the blacksmith's. In Dartmouth, they call him Archibald's Icelander."

"I have heard that in Dartmouth there is an Icelander
named Ármann," I said.

"That will be the same man," said Miller. "Likely there is
only the one Icelander in Dartmouth.

Mark Miller and I travelled for two days, a distance of fifty
miles or more. We spent the night with a kind farm family

near Grand Lake. We were given good food and a comfortable bed, but still I dreamed an unpleasant dream. I felt that Bay, our horse, had been frightened and had gone completely out of control. He had run away with the cart, the two of us holding on for dear life. I felt that we were crashing over some dangerous cliffs down by the sea coast. I woke up terrified and was unable to relax enough to sleep again. In the morning I told Mr. Miller about my dream, but he only smiled and said, "Don't worry about dreams." But the effect of the dream stayed with me all day, and I worried all the rest of the way to Dartmouth. We arrived in Halifax about six o'clock in the evening. There was a cold, miserable fog creeping over the Bay so my first impressions of the town were not very pleasant. Actually on a bright sunny day the view of the city is beautiful, especially in the summertime.

When we arrived at the Oswald residence, about half a mile out of town, I was seized with a feeling of dread. I felt that the house looked so dreary. Before I left home and along the way, I had been imagining that this house would be big and grand looking, but now I saw that it was just the opposite. Actually, it was fairly large but very plain and in a state of disrepair. The house was down in a deep ravine near the sea, cut off and lonely. Between the house and the town was a high hill, which made it seem all the lonelier out there. Inside, the house was no more pleasant than outside. Although there were many rooms both upstairs and downstairs, they were not in use and were empty except for three rooms, which were living quarters for the old couple. These three rooms were sparsely furnished at that but were clean and tidy.

I was well received, to be sure. Mr. and Mrs. Oswald were

cheerful and good-natured and tried their best to make me feel welcome. Their attitude toward me remained the same throughout my stay there. They were always considerate and fair. They were both in their sixties. Mr. Oswald was a small man who was lame and walked with a cane. His wife was small, too, and thin and delicate in appearance.

From the first time I set foot inside the door, I suffered from homesickness, but the worst time was the first two weeks. I made it very clear to Mark Miller the morning after we arrived there that I wanted to go back home with him. Of course, he would not hear of that. Then he left the three of us together.

Of course the old couple were aware from the start that I was not happy there, although I tried not to show it. They never left me alone that first day but took turns talking to me and showing me what work I should do. They had a horse, two cows and some chickens for me to look after, and at the back of the house was a large garden that needed a good deal of attention.

Mr. Oswald was forever ready to read from the Scottish poets Robert Burns, James Hogg and David Sillar. He knew dozens of poems from memory. Most of them were written in Scottish dialect, which made it difficult for me to understand them, and therefore I did not enjoy them very much. The old woman often talked with me about her son, Robert, and showed me different things that belonged to him, among them some toys that he had kept since he was a little boy.

"These are my boy's toys," she said. "He was always good and willing when he was young and he will always be conscientious and good. But now he is at sea. May God bless and protect him."

I found more comfort in talking to her than her husband, partly because he spoke with a stronger Scottish accent. But I sensed that her thoughts were always with Robert, her son, who was so dear to her. I was sure that she yearned for his homecoming as much as I yearned to get home to my own mother. I felt that this realization eased my pain a little.

Shortly after I arrived, I asked Mr. Oswald whether he knew of any Icelanders in Dartmouth. He did not know of any. I told him that I had heard that there was an Icelander by the name of Ármann who worked for a blacksmith by the name of Archibald. Mr. Oswald said that he knew of a blacksmith in Dartmouth named Archibald but he had no idea who his workmen were. He said that he would inquire about it next time he went to town.

As it turned out, he did not have to inquire for shortly afterwards an old man from Dartmouth came to visit Mr. and Mrs. Oswald. They knew him well. His name was John Williams and he was a gardener. When he saw me he asked Mr. Oswald where I came from. As soon as he was told that I was an Icelander, he started telling us about an Icelandic man who had spent considerable time with Allan Archibald, the blacksmith.

"What is his name?" asked Mr. Oswald.

"I don't know," answered Williams. "He is usually called the Icelander or Archibald's Icelander. He is said to be a good workman, equally good with wood or iron. I have been told that in his spare time he is building a boat big enough for four passengers, and some say that he is planning to travel by himself all the way to Iceland as soon as it is seaworthy. He is not content to stay in America."

"This is ridiculous," said Mr. Oswald. "No one would set

out in a small boat by himself across the Atlantic."

"Men say that is what he has in mind," repeated Williams.

A few days later Mr. Oswald had an errand in Dartmouth and asked me to come along with him. I gratefully accepted the offer. When we got into town he pointed to a blacksmith shop down by the sea.

"That is Archibald's shop," he said. "You may wait for me there while I do my business in the store over yonder. I know that you would like to meet your countryman. You must not waste his time, but you may invite him over to our place on Sunday if you like."

I was ever so grateful to Mr. Oswald for his offer. I walked directly to the blacksmith shop, stopped in front of the door and looked in. The shop was large and three men were working busily. They were all big, strong men, but one seemed bigger than the others did and I took for granted that this was the boss, Allan Archibald. I walked over to him as he stood beside his anvil and asked him whether there was an Icelandic man there by the name of Ármann.

"What do you want with him?" asked the big man good-naturedly after studying me for a moment. I noticed then that he was fair-haired, blue-eyed, with rather a long face, and he had a kindly expression.

"I am Icelandic," I said, "and I would like to speak to him."

"Really!" he said. "And what is your name?"

I told him my name and that I was the errand boy for Mr. Oswald, who lived half a mile north of town, but my parents were in the Icelandic settlement in Mooseland Hills.

"I am the man you are looking for," he said in Icelandic, and smiled at me.

"Is your name Ármann?" I asked.

"Yes, my name is Ármann. I am Icelandic and I am your cousin." He patted my shoulder as he said this.

"Are you related to my Dad?" I asked, "or perhaps you are related to my mother?"

"I am related to both of them, and that's why I am your cousin. What did you want to talk to me about?" Ármann looked over his shoulder back into the shop as he said this.

"I would just like to speak to you in Icelandic about something—about anything—because you are Icelandic," I said hesitantly.

"I am pressed for time as you can see," he said kindly. "Could you come back on Sunday afternoon? Or, if you would rather, I could come to see you."

"Yes, that is what I would prefer," I said. "Do you know the way to the house where I stay?"

"Yes. The Oswald house is just north of the hill. I will come on Sunday afternoon."

"Then I will leave you. God bless you," I said.

"God be with you, cousin," he smiled as he raised his hand to say goodbye. "God be with you always!"

Then I walked over to the store where Mr. Oswald was buying tea and sugar and I went home with him. My heart felt lighter because I had found an Icelander who was also a cousin of mine.

Next Sunday, shortly after noon, Ármann came to see me as he had promised. Mr. and Mrs. Oswald received him courteously. He spoke to them for a few minutes in reasonably good English. He was neatly dressed and had shaved that morning. He looked younger than he did when I saw him in the shop and he seemed even bigger. He was a full six feet tall and well muscled.

After he talked to Mr. Oswald for a few minutes, he asked me to come for a walk down to the sea with him. I was ready to do that.

"It is good to walk by the sea when one is feeling sad or homesick," said Ármann. We walked back and forth along the beach for a while and then we sat down on a rock.

"I am very homesick," I said.

"Aren't Mr. and Mrs. Oswald good to you?" he asked me.

"Yes, they are good to me," I said. "But still I long to go. I can't speak to them about it."

"Mr. Oswald told me just now that you would be with them while their son is away. He will be back in four months. That is not such a long time.

"It seems like forever to me," I said.

"Dear cousin," said Ármann, slapping me on the shoulder, "it would not look good if you left these kind, old people before their son comes home. That would not be in the spirit of a good Icelander. Everyone who knows these people says that they are good and kind. They are poor now, so they say, because they helped people out more than they could afford. If I was in your position, I would try to take the place of their son while Robert is away."

"I will try to do that," I said, "but I long to go home to see my mother and I can hardly think of anything but my family and the little log house in the settlement in Mooseland Hills. That house is so warm and bright, but here I feel everything is so cold and dark."

"I know what homesickness is," said Ármann after a short pause. "I was smitten with homesickness as soon as I came to this country. And six years have now gone by."

"Did you want to see your mother?" I asked.

"I wanted to go home to Iceland," said Ármann in a low voice.

"Were you very homesick?" I asked.

"Yes, so much that I could neither sleep nor eat at first."

"Why did you not go home then?" I asked.

"I would have gone home if there had been a way but I did not have the means," said Ármann quietly. "Jobs were hard to find, and the pay was low and this has not changed. I spent some time in the United States and then I went to Barrie, Ontario, and worked at a sawmill. When I came to Halifax, my plan was to find work to pay for my passage home. In Halifax, I met Mr. Archibald and I came back to Dartmouth with him. I have been with him ever since. I always long to get home, but homesickness does not affect me now the way it did the first year. Now I am able to control my feelings. One can learn to handle homesickness."

"Is there some medicine that will treat that sickness?" I asked.

"Yes. There is a medicine that each man is given," answered Ármann. "Have you heard the story of the little prince in the East, who was adopted by a mighty ruler in India? That was long, long ago. At first the prince was so homesick that he could not even talk to people. Then his adopted mother came to him and told him the story of the prince who freed the seven sisters from the spell that bound them, but she told him that he would have to tell her the same story the following day. The little prince listened so attentively that he was able to tell the story to his adopted mother the next day. Then she agreed to tell him another story but asked him to remember it well so that he could tell it to her again. For a hundred days she told him a new story each day, and each day he had to be prepared to tell her the story she had told the day before. Gradually he began to feel better and better until finally he overcame his homesickness—in a hundred days."

"This is not a true story," I said.

"It could well be that it is not a true story," said Ármann, smiling, but the story of Egill Skallagrímsson is certainly true. His son Böðvar was lost at sea, shortly after his other young son, Gunnar, had died. Egill was so overwhelmed by his sorrow that life seemed utterly impossible and he vowed to starve himself to death. But þorgerður, his daughter, asked him to write a poem in memory of Böðvar.

He was reluctant at first because he felt that he could not compose even if he tried, but he finally agreed. He wrote the famous poem *Sonatorrek* in memory of Böðvar and Gunnar. It was very difficult for him to begin, but he seemed to improve with every stanza. By the time the poem was finished, his state of mind had improved so much that he gave up his idea of starving himself to death. He had found his own medicine to soothe his sorrow and his mental agony."

"But he was a poet," I said.

"All men have some poetic gifts," said Ármann, "and often these are easily developed in the young, especially in young people about your age. You should write a long poem to drive the homesickness out of your mind."

"That would be impossible for me," I said. "I have never so much as put together a single verse."

"You could still try, cousin," said Ármann, and he gave me a reassuring hug. "Whenever you want you can let your imagination take you into Álfheim, the home of all the good fairies. You can let your imagination create a wonderland.

You can build cities and castles, call forth flocks of beautiful elves and human beings as well, whole armies of heroes and princes. You could write a long ballad about this wonderland of yours. You should start right today."

I said nothing.

After a while we stood up and walked back to the house. When Ármann took his leave, he said to me, "Come and see me next Sunday. I will be in the big shed just south of the blacksmith shop. I am going to show you something."

Next Sunday, just before noon, I went to Dartmouth and made my way directly to the shed south of Mr. Archibald's blacksmith shop. Ármann was sitting on a bench beside the door when I arrived. He was reading a book but he put it away as soon as he noticed me.

"Have you started your poem?" he asked, after I sat down on the bench beside him. I did not answer but I took a piece of paper from my pocket and passed it to him. My face reddened. There were three verses written on that page, if you could call them that. I had spent a whole week trying to put them together.

Ármann read the verses again and again, seemingly with interest and enjoyment. He smiled from time to time and scratched his head a little.

"This is a good beginning," he said finally. "Now just keep on, and write a long poem. You could call it *Fairy Tales in Rhyme*. You have to be careful with the metre," and then he gave a few pointers in that regard.

"I think that I will never be able to add anything to these verses," I said. "I have such a hard time getting the sound right and keeping the rhyme scheme. I can never find the right word."

"It gets easier and easier as time goes on if you don't get discouraged," said Ármann. "You are like Egill Skallagrímsson when he started writing his poem *Ransom*. He could not write because the owl sat hooting outside his window, until Arinbjörn chased it away and sat beside the window himself. In your window sits a big owl that bothers you and gives you no peace; her name is Homesickness. I have decided that I will be your Arninbjörn and I will chase that wretched owl away. I believe I can do just that. Come into the shed with me. I have something here to show you."

We walked into the large shed. It was big and roomy, and there were a lot of interesting things to look at.

"This is my poem," said Ármann, and pointed to a boat in the middle of the shop. The boat was new, a beautiful little ship and of sturdy construction.

"I have been working on it for almost two years. Now the work is nearly finished. This boat is called a four passenger but it could just as well be a six passenger. The mast is beside the wall there and I just have some small items to finish. I have been doing this in my spare time so that I would feel better. Mr. Archibald has supplied most of the materials."

"Is it Mr. Archibald's boat?" I asked.

"No, it is my boat."

"Is it true that you are planning to travel all the way to Iceland in this boat?" I asked.

"Have you heard that?" asked Ármann, amused.

"I heard that you were building a boat and that you planned to use it to travel to Iceland," I said.

"Yes, people talk a lot."

"It would be impossible to travel all that way in an open boat," I said.

"What about our ancestors? The ships that carried them across the Atlantic were not very big."

"But they had many men," I continued. "One man alone in a small boat could not travel across the Atlantic to Iceland."

"Yes, if he was strong and brave and had learned good seamanship."

"Are you really planning to go to Iceland on this boat?" I studied Ármann's face.

"I haven't decided yet, but who knows, maybe this boat will take me home."

"Do you want very badly to get there?" I asked.

"Yes, I am always thinking of home."

"Do you not like this country?"

"Yes, in many ways I like it here. There is gold here, beautiful forests and good people. But still, I want to go home."

"Would you want to go to Iceland if the people there did not speak Icelandic any more, but some other language instead?"

"Under those circumstances I would not wish quite so much to go."

"Would you still want to go to Iceland if all the Icelandic people were in America and continued to speak Icelandic here?"

"That would make it difficult," said Ármann. "I would like best to hear Icelandic spoken by people in Iceland. The land, the people and the language are one as far as I am concerned and I cannot do without them. All these, and more, demand my return. But come, have a look at my boat."

So I looked over his boat with interest and I admired the workmanship. In my eyes it was magnificent, nothing short of a masterpiece.

That day I had lunch at the home of Mr. Archibald. I was well received and they invited me to come back whenever I liked. This pleased me very much, and I was feeling much better when I returned to the Oswalds' house that evening.

Throughout the summer I met Ármann every weekend. Either he came to visit me early in the afternoon or I went to Dartmouth and enjoyed dinner with the Archibald family. If the weather was good we always went for a walk down by the ocean. Ármann enjoyed that. He told me stories and often recited poems, which I think he had written himself. And at these times he encouraged me to continue with my epic poem, but I never got very far with that.

On a Friday morning at the beginning of September, Ármann came to see me. He was dressed in his best clothes.

"Now I am leaving for Iceland," he said.

I was surprised. "You're not going in your boat, are you?"

"Yes, in a way," he said and smiled. "I sold it on Monday and got a good price for it, so I can pay for my passage with that money. A wealthy merchant from Halifax bought it and sailed on it to Bedford the day before yesterday. He is very pleased with it and is calling it *The Viking*. I am travelling with a ship that leaves from Halifax for England tomorrow morning, but I have to board this evening. I came to say goodbye to you."

"I am going to walk into town with you and say goodbye to you there."

"I would like that," said Ármann, and I could see that he would be glad to have my company.

So I asked Mr. Oswald's permission to go and, when he heard that Ármann was leaving for Iceland, he said that I could have the day off. And so I spent the day with him, his last day in America! I felt I had so much to talk about. One of the many questions I asked him was this: "How are we related? You told me I was your cousin."

He answered, "All Icelanders are my relatives. You are an Icelander, so you are related to me."

The last question I asked was: "Why do you feel you have to go back to Iceland when you are getting along so well here and everyone likes you so much?"

"As I have often told you this summer," he answered me, "there are many things that call me home. I'll tell you one thing, cousin. There is a grave in a little churchyard out in the country that I have to look after."

"Was it not there when you left Iceland?" I asked.

"No," he said, and I knew from his voice that he could not talk about it any more.

Around noon Mr. Archibald and I accompanied Ármann on the ferry to Halifax. We went with him right out to the ship and said goodbye to him there. I thanked him for all that he had done for me and I was sorry to see him leave. Mr. Archibald handed him a small parcel and said, "Good luck to you! You are a good man!"

Mr. and Mrs. Oswald were always kind to me. They gave me a new set of clothes and a few dollars as well. Their son came back just one month after Ármann left for Iceland. A few days later he took me back to the settlement in Mooseland Hills, back to the log cabin and my family.

MABEL MCISAAC

All Icelandic people who have spent any time in Nova Scotia have heard of the Musquodoboit district. In the middle of that area there is a place called Cooks Brook, and just west of that is the Chaswood Valley. Mabel McIsaac lived in that valley. Her house was on the west side, just south of the Duncan River, which rises in the hills on the north and rushes down the slopes. When the snow melts in the spring the river becomes a torrent, and then the logs are floated down toward the sawmill. As I remember it, the Chaswood Valley was very beautiful, but there were only a few houses there. The church stood on a little knoll in the middle of the valley about half a mile from the graveyard, which was right beside the main road. There was a store about half a mile further south. Around the graveyard was a low stone fence, and around the fence there was a row of tall and stately elm trees. On moonlit nights when the wind was up, the trees cast eerie shadows on the graves.

Mabel McIsaac always passed the graveyard on her way to the store. I met her for the first time in the summer of 1878. That summer I was errand boy for Mr. Donald, who was the Justice of the Peace. I was twelve years old and Mabel looked to be about twenty. On that day, she was coming from the store, carrying her basket on her arm. She was barefoot, tall and strongly built, with raven-black hair that fell in curls around her shoulders. On her head she wore a wide, straw hat. She had a high forehead and large, hazel eyes. I cannot say that she was really pretty. She had a doleful expression on her face. She walked along rather slowly and stopped now and again to study the wildflowers that grew by the roadside. She was singing bits of a melancholy folksong that was popular in Nova Scotia at that time. Her voice was quite pleasant. I greeted her when I met her.

"Good day, boy," she said, as she passed me.

I turned round and saw that she had also turned. Our eyes met briefly. I thought her eyes looked a little strange. Then I continued on my way and she carried on in the other direction. Soon she resumed her singing.

When I returned home that day, I stopped near the graveyard and I saw that Mabel was there. She was bent over a grave in the southeast corner. When she noticed me she looked startled, then hurried out of the gate and off to her home. After she left, I walked into the graveyard toward the grave that she had visited. It was not a new grave for it was covered with thick grass. There was no headstone or marker of any kind, but two evergreen branches arranged in a cross had recently been placed there. Some freshly picked flowers formed the letters H and M.

Almost every week during that summer I saw Mabel in the graveyard. She always attended to the same grave, brought fresh flowers and every now and again brought new green branches, which she laid in a cross. When she saw me, she always hurried home without speaking to me. At first I thought she might be visiting her father's grave because I had heard that he had died when Mabel was a small child. Later I learned that his grave was the Atlantic Ocean.

As I mentioned before, Mabel and her mother lived in a little house just south of the Duncan River. Around the house there were a few rows of apple trees, and below the house was an old barn and four elm trees. I remember that my friends and I thought this barn was very odd because one end was red, the other end was blue, and both sides were very light in colour. The women were rather poor but they had managed on their own without assistance from others. They were both hard-working, like most of the Scottish countrywomen in Nova Scotia. They did not hesitate to tackle outdoor chores. I did not hear much about these two, but everything I heard said about them was good.

"Mrs. McIsaac is an honest, hard-working woman," I heard my employer say one day, "and Mabel is a capable worker and has a good heart, but she is a little off here," he said, as he pointed to his forehead.

One day I was sent on an errand to the home of Mr. Higgins who lived on the ridge west of the McIsaacs'. He was hospitable, and our people from the settlement often stayed overnight at his house when they had to travel to Stewiacke. On the way back, I stopped at the McIsaacs' house because they lived right beside the road, and I asked for a drink of water.

"I haven't seen this boy before," said Mrs. McIsaac when she brought my drink. She was a small woman with sharp, black eyes.

"I am an errand boy for Mr. Donald," I told her.

"And you have just started there?" asked Mrs. McIsaac.

"I came this spring," I said.

"Have you seen him before, Mabel?" asked Mrs. McIsaac, as she looked toward her daughter.

"Yes," said Mabel, and she stared across the valley as if she were looking at something interesting.

"And you never told me that Donald had a new errand boy?"

"No," said Mabel, and she turned and looked toward the ridge as if she saw someone coming from that direction.

"Where did Mr. Donald find such a smart-looking boy?"

"I don't know," said Mabel, and she turned her gaze back across the valley.

"I'm from Mooseland Hills," I said.

"From Mooseland Hills? Did I hear right?" said Mrs. McIsaac. "I thought there were only Icelandic settlers there."

"And I am Icelandic," I said, quite proudly.

"And you never told me that he was Icelandic?" said Mrs. McIsaac to her daughter.

"I did not know that," said Mabel. She looked at me closely for a few moments and she seemed particularly sorrowful. All of a sudden she left us and walked out towards the river. Her mother watched her leave and then she said to me, "So you are Icelandic?"

"Yes, I was born in Iceland," I answered.

"Then he was likely Icelandic, too," she said, after pausing to think for a while.

"Who?" I asked.

"Oh, that doesn't matter," she said, "but do stop and get a drink whenever you are passing by." I thanked her, said goodbye and continued on my way.

A few days later I met Mabel on the road down in the valley. By this time it was late summer but still it was quite a hot day. "Good day, boy," she said, as she set her basket down on the road.

"Good day," I said, and I lifted my hat.

"It is hot," she said, as she wiped the perspiration off her forehead.

"Yes it is," I said, as I pulled out my handkerchief. There was a long silence. She looked down and she kicked at the sand with her bare foot.

"Did you know him?" she asked, finally, as she stared into my face.

"Who?" I asked.

"The man whom my mother asked about," she said.

"She did not ask me about anyone," I said.

"Did she not ask you?" she said, and her eyes grew big and her colour changed.

"No," I said.

"Goodbye, boy." She picked up her basket and left.

"Goodbye," I said as I watched her go. I remembered Mr. Donald's words.

"She is not quite right," he had said, and he had pointed to his forehead. Now I thought I understood him.

Later that fall, I stopped again at the McIsaacs'. The mother invited me into the kitchen. The furnishings were very simple, but the place was very clean and well cared for. Mabel sat beside a window with a view of the valley. She was busy with some sewing and as she sewed, she kept looking out of the window, as if she was expecting someone to come up the hill. Her mother walked over to her and whispered in her ear. Mabel did not seem to pay any attention because she kept on sewing and looking out of the window from time to time. Finally, she got up, walked to a cupboard and took out a little chest. She opened the chest, handed a large key to her mother and went back to her sewing.

"I'm going to show you something," Mrs. McIsaac said to me. She showed me into a little room. In it was an old-fashioned bed and a little table. In one corner was a large green *koffort* of Icelandic design. Two large letters, H and M, were painted on either side of the keyhole.

"Have you seen a trunk like this before?" she asked.

"Yes," I said. "My parents have two trunks very similar to this except for the colour and the initials." She opened up the trunk with the key that her daughter had given her.

"Have you seen clothes of this style before?" she asked, as she pointed to the open chest.

"Yes," I said in amazement. "These must have belonged to an Icelander." In the trunk was men's clothing made from good, dark Icelandic homespun. There were also brown socks and two pairs of light-blue mittens. There were sheep-skin slippers with fine, knitted insoles. The letters H and M were embroidered into the insoles. There was a copy of the New Testament in Icelandic. I saw an inscription on the front page that said, "Full ownership of this book belongs to Sigurlaug Bjarnadóttir." There were a few other books and a letter which a woman had written to her sister. I could see from the envelope that it had been sent by mail. In the bottom of the chest there were a few old and rather rusty carpenter's tools and a few pages from an old Icelandic story-book. I studied all these items carefully but nothing told me who the owner was. All I knew was that he was Icelandic, and I believed that H and M must be his initials. When I had studied everything in the chest, Mrs. McIsaac put the things back, just as they had been before, and she locked the trunk.

"Who owns this?" I asked.

"The man who died here owned it," she said, and she looked at the bed. "He said he was Icelandic but most did not believe that. Folk did not know anything about Icelandic people at that time, and we thought that they resembled Eskimos. He was tall and well built, with golden hair and beautiful blue eyes. He was here two years before Icelandic settlers arrived in Mooseland. He came directly from Halifax. Some thought that he was not Icelandic at all, but in fact a deserter from the army because he moved like a soldier, so straight and tall. The priest said he looked Norwegian or Danish because of his blond hair. He found it hard to speak English but he was able to understand what was said to him. Men called him Harry because they could not pronounce his name. I remember that the first three letters were "Hal" because he wrote his name for me once. He worked in Cameron's Lumber Camp up in the hills. He was said to be a good workman and all the fellows liked him.

He was in an accident in 1875 when the logs were being floated down the Duncan River. I did not know just how it happened, but he was hurt while he was doing that work. He had internal injuries. He was brought to our house because the accident occurred nearby. He was bedridden all summer and then, in the fall, he died, here in this bed. Mabel was his nurse and she has been strange ever since he died. He was buried in the southeast corner of the graveyard and all of Cameron's men attended the funeral, and ourselves, too. He wanted to tell us something before he died, but we could not understand what he said. It was something about his mother. Poor Mabel has put flowers on his grave every summer. She had become so ... but what am I saying? She is Scottish through and through, and Scots never forget those they have loved. When the Icelandic settlers came to Mooseland Hills, we asked the priest to inquire whether anyone was acquainted with this man or knew of his people, but it seems that he has learned nothing. We will keep his trunk until some of his relatives claim it."

"You don't remember his last name?" I asked.

"No," she said, "but the first letter was M and the name ended in "son." He was always known as Harry. Please try to find out who he was and where his relatives are and let us know. I know he tried to tell us something about his mother just before he died. With tears in his eyes, he touched my hand. He was always pleasant and thankful for anything that was done for him and he didn't complain. It was just so hard to understand him. Halfway through the summer he seemed to be improving, and he got up for a few days and sat in the shade of the big apple tree out there. Then he got worse and he died in the fall. Poor Mabel has been so strange ever since."

I saw that Mrs. McIsaac wiped her eyes. Then we walked out of the bedroom, but Mabel had disappeared. I said good-bye to Mrs. McIsaac and left for home. I met Mabel down the road. She carried some evergreen branches in her hand.

"Do you know whether his mother is still living?" she asked.

"No, I don't know," I had to tell her.

"Try to find out for me, please," she said. I promised to try.

"God bless you, boy," she said. "God bless you."

I returned to Mooseland just before Christmas and I did not go back to the Chaswood Valley until June 1882, when I was about to leave for Winnipeg. I spent a day with the

Donald family. Then I learned that Mrs. McIsaac had died, but Mabel was still in the house and her aunt had moved in with her, along with a son who was disabled.

I visited Mabel and she received me well. She asked me right away whether I had any information for her and I had to admit that I had none.

"I want to show you something," she said. We walked down to the graveyard. Now there was a small marble headstone on the grave in the southeast corner. On it was lettered "HM, 26 years, born in Iceland".

"I did this," she said, "so that his grave would not be lost. He had no one here. If you ever find out where his relatives are, let them know where they can find his grave, but you don't have to mention me."

This was the last time that I saw Mabel, and the last time that I visited the graveyard in Chaswood Valley.

This story was first published in Winnipeg in Almanak, *1906. A note explains: "Mabel died two years ago. She never married and folk said she was 'strange.' Few knew that she carried a deep sorrow that she never wanted to forget. There is no marker on her grave, but a stone marks the grave of the Icelander. Who he was I do not know, but I do know that no one was a more loyal friend than Mabel was to him."*

EYVINDUR

In 1878, four new families came from Iceland to settle in the Mooseland Hills. On the ship was a young man who was travelling alone. He called himself simply Eyvindur Atli. Atli may have been one of his Christian names, likely inherited from a grandfather. Eyvindur accompanied the four families to the settlement, but he only stopped there for two or three days because he was anxious to find some work.

He was barely twenty years old, of average height and rather slim. He had reddish hair and hazel eyes. He was good-looking and mannerly in a quiet way. He was told that he might find employment in the mining town of Tangier, which was about thirty miles away. The other alternative might be to look for work with farmers in the Musquodoboit Valley, for it was early August and harvest would soon be on the way. He said that he preferred farm work to mining.

Some men from the settlement accompanied him to the valley and acted as spokesmen for him. After a few unsuccessful inquiries, they decided to call on a farmer named Balfour. Mr. Balfour was of Scottish descent, about fifty years old. He was a fine-looking man and was held in high regard by all the Icelandic people in Mooseland Hills. He had been helpful to them ever since their arrival. In their first year in Nova Scotia, Balfour had taken the trouble to visit them and to explain many things, especially with regard to agriculture and gardening. Each year he continued to call on them in spring and in fall, and he helped them in any way he could.

Balfour lived in a beautiful valley that we called Maple Valley and that runs eastward from the larger Musquodoboit Valley. Through Maple Valley runs a rapid river called Millbrook. On its banks were two small mills; one was a sawmill and the other a grist mill. On both sides of the river stretched excellent hay fields and, higher up the slopes, were well-kept farms, eleven farmhouses as I recall. Each house was surrounded by a grove of apple trees, and each of the farms had long barns and sheds for storing hay. There were large vegetable gardens and fields of grain, usually oats, barley or buckwheat. Balfour's house was higher up the slope than the other houses and, from his home, there was a good view of all the other homes in the valley. His land reached all the way from the river to the ridge.

Mr. Balfour greeted Eyvindur kindly and said that he was sure that he could find work with farmers in the neighbourhood. He offered to take Eyvindur around and introduce him. In the meantime, he said that he would be welcome to stay at his house until he found a job. This offer was gratefully accepted.

Eyvindur helped with the harvest at two farms that autumn. He soon learned how to use the sickle and proved to be capable and hard-working. During the next winter, he stayed at Balfour's home and was treated like one of the family. Balfour's two sons, one twelve and the other fifteen, quickly became fond of Eyvindur and doubtless helped him learn English very quickly. Eyvindur and the older boy visited the settlement between Christmas and New Year's.

Their errand was to fetch Eyvindur's *koffort*, which had been left there in the fall. Eyvindur returned for a visit at Easter in 1879, when he learned that most of the settlers planned to leave Mooseland Hills as soon as possible and relocate in the Red River Valley. Eyvindur determined that he would go too, and he resolved that he would work hard all summer and earn enough to make that move before the next winter set in.

He told Balfour about his decision and Balfour placed him with his neighbour, a Mr. Lang, who was a well-established farmer. Eyvindur was to work for Lang for three months—July, August and September—and the wages plus board and room would be fifteen dollars per month. Eyvindur started his new job at the beginning of July. At the same time, I was hired as an errand boy and I was expected to stay there until school started in the settlement that fall. I was thirteen years old and I had lived in Nova Scotia for almost four years.

During that summer, I got to know Eyvindur quite well. We were often together, especially when we were making hay or cutting grain. Eyvindur was always pleasant and he often told me stories and recited poetry. Short verses, *visur*, were his favourites. He often talked about Mr. and Mrs. Balfour and said that he owed them a debt of gratitude because they had shown him such kindness and goodwill. He also told me about the sons who had been so nice to him. Every Sunday while Eyvindur worked for Mr. Lang, he would walk over to the Balfours' place and visit with them for a while. "I would like to call him Baldur—Baldur the Good," said Eyvindur, because he has goodwill to everyone and, in turn, everyone thinks well of him."

Our employer, Mr. Lang, was himself a fine man, hard-working and practical. He had built up an excellent farm and, besides that, he was a blacksmith and he spent quite a lot of time in his shop. He liked Eyvindur and thought he was a good worker. He always called him "lad," but said that he would grow into a good man one day.

Haying was almost complete, and most of the hay had been stowed away in the barn or in stacks near the farm buildings. Then Eyvindur asked one day if he could make a bed for himself in the hayloft and sleep there. He said it would be cooler there than in the house. The Langs said that that was up to him, but they did wonder why he would choose to sleep in the hayloft rather than in a good bed upstairs in their house.

One morning when the grain fields in the valley were ripening, Lang came to talk to Eyvindur and me while we were repairing a fence around the garden. "Have you noticed, lad," he said to Eyvindur, "that Balfour's barley has turned colour and his buckwheat is ready, too? In fact, it looks to me as if they have started to cut the buckwheat. What do you think, lad?" Lang pointed in the direction of Balfour's fields. Up at the ridge there was quite a large grain field and, sure enough, from where we stood it was plain to see that some cutting had been done there.

At that time, all grain was cut with a sickle in Maple Valley and in Mooseland Hills. Sheaves of barley or oats were tied with straw, and the grain was threshed out with a flail in the barnyard later in the fall. The buckwheat was not tied but was raised up in small stooks in the fields, and the grain was threshed out there.

Eyvindur looked over in the direction of Balfour's farm-yard, which was about a mile away. "I see that the barley field is turning golden. In fact, I had noticed that yesterday when I walked over there," he said.

"Our friend Balfour is a good farmer," said Lang. "He has the best grain fields in the valley and he is always the first one to seed buckwheat and barley in the spring and the first to start cutting every fall. He will be ahead of us as usual. Don't you see the stooks of buckwheat in the western part of the field?"

"I don't see that clearly," said Eyvindur, and put up a hand to shade his eyes.

"Don't you see, lad, that they are cutting the buckwheat?"

"That could be," said Eyvindur.

"Yes. There are two of them cutting, likely Balfour's boys. Don't you see that, lad?"

"Yes, I think I see some activity," said Eyvindur.

"Well, lads," said Lang. "First thing tomorrow morning we'll have to start cutting my buckwheat. We'll have to keep going or we'll be way behind Balfour. His field is quite a bit bigger than ours, mind you."

This conversation took place on a Monday morning. Early Tuesday morning, Eyvindur and I started cutting Lang's buckwheat. Lang came out to see us about nine o'clock and he brought a newly sharpened sickle. He came straight from his blacksmith shop. "Our friend Balfour has made good progress since yesterday morning," Lang said to Eyvindur. "Look at the hillside, lad. They have cut the whole piece west of the footpath."

Eyvindur looked eastward into the hill. "That is so," he said, and he set to work again.

"In this warm weather the buckwheat will start shedding if it is not cut quickly, as our friend over there knows full

well," said Lang. "We'll have to follow his example and finish cutting before the week is over." For the rest of the day,
all three of us worked together in the field.

On Wednesday, Lang came out to the field earlier than the
day before and we thought that he seemed to be in quite a
rush. "This is no time to sit around," he said to Eyvindur.
"Our friend Balfour is getting further ahead of us. At this
rate, he will be finished before the weekend and still there
are just two of them working, likely Balfour himself and the
older boy. Look eastward, lad, and see if you can see more
than two men working in the field."

Eyvindur looked eastward.

"I see only two men," he said.

"Those two men certainly make headway," muttered
Lang, as he set to work. We three laboured at a steady pace
all day.

On Thursday, Eyvindur and I went out very early and
Lang joined us shortly after. "I guess we'll have to keep moving with our cutting today," he said. "If we don't watch out,
we will not finish our small field by the time Balfour finishes
his big one. Say, don't you think those are Balfour's boys
working over there today?"

"I see two men," said Eyvindur. "Undoubtedly one of
them will be Balfour himself."

"I don't think so," said Lang. "This morning I thought I
saw him walk around his field and, when he was walking
toward the house, two men met him on their way to the field.
They were clearly smaller than he was."

"Is that so?" said Eyvindur.

"They were his sons," said Lang.

"Likely," said Eyvindur.

Then we got busy and we worked hard until sunset, except for an hour's rest at noon.

On Friday morning Eyvindur and I started out to the field earlier than usual, and Lang had already sharpened the sickles.

"Balfour's boys are further ahead of us than they were last night," said Lang, as he looked over the field. "Our friend must have been out all night and worked hard, at that, because there was a full moon. Balfour knows that when the weather is so dry and warm it is better to cut the buckwheat at night than during the day."

"Well, that may be," said Eyvindur.

All that day we worked hard, and when we quit in the evening there was only a small strip of Lang's field left uncut. "We have made good progress today," said Lang, "and, if all goes well, we should finish by noon tomorrow. Balfour's boys are almost finished, too. They have only a small corner left to do. No doubt they will finish well before noon and be done before we are." We looked up into the hillside and we noted that, indeed, the Balfours had only a small piece left to finish.

"They started a whole day before we did," said Eyvindur.

"That is true," said Lang, "but their field is much bigger than ours."

Then came Saturday. Eyvindur and I went out earlier than ever. Lang soon joined us and this time he was smiling. "Well, lad," he said to Eyvindur, "now it is clear that Balfour has worked all night every day this week because he has finished cutting the buckwheat. He doesn't let the grass grow under his feet. Just take a look over there, lad." Sure enough, Balfour's buckwheat had all been cut during the night.

"Well, look at that!" said Eyvindur, happily. "The boys have finished ahead of us."

"Yes, the boys and their father," said Lang. "It would be hard to outdo that one."

Just before noon we finished cutting Lang's buckwheat. In the afternoon, Eyvindur and I returned to the fencing that we had left on Monday night. On Saturday evening, two farmers from the neighbourhood came to talk to Mr. Lang. They told him that Balfour had been sick and had been bedridden for almost a week and he was still far from well.

"How can this be?" asked Lang. "Hasn't he been cutting grain all this week?"

"No," said one of the visitors. "His boys started cutting the buckwheat on Monday morning and they finished this morning but they still have to cut the barley and the oats and to thresh the buckwheat. We'll all get together and help them right after the weekend."

"Am I to believe that Balfour's boys alone cut all that buckwheat in five days? Someone must have been helping them," said Lang.

"Mr. and Mrs. Balfour told us today," said the other visitor, "that the boys had noticed on several mornings that someone had been working in the field and had cut a big strip during the night."

"Who could that have been?" asked Lang.

"The Balfours don't know who it could have been," was the reply. "It may have been either MacPherson, Balfour's brother-in-law, or Sutherland. They are the closest neighbours on the east side of the farm."

"This is very odd," said Lang.

Nothing more was said that day, but next Monday and

also Tuesday and Wednesday every farm in Maple Valley sent a man to help cut the oats and the barley at Balfours'. The work was completed quickly. Some cut, some tied the bundles and some threshed out the buckwheat and moved the grain into bins. Lang did not go himself but he sent Eyvindur to work there for three days. The men who worked there commented on Eyvindur's endurance and his contribution to the work.

For a while, people were trying to guess who had cut the buckwheat while others slept. Most thought that MacPherson or Sutherland, or the two working together, had done it. Lang said he had some ideas but he mentioned no names. I had my own idea. I had noted one morning while we were working on Lang's buckwheat that Eyvindur had a bandaged finger on his left hand. It often happened that men would cut a finger on their left hand when they were rushing too much during harvest.

"It was you," I said to Eyvindur one time when men were discussing the mystery.

"Nonsense," he said, so I said no more.

I went back to the settlement in mid September and that was the last time I ever saw Maple Valley. Eyvindur did not go to Winnipeg that autumn as he had planned. He worked for Mr. Lang until Christmastime and then he returned to Balfours' and stayed with them until May of 1880. Then he left to go to the Red River Valley.

I saw Mr. Balfour once more, in the fall of 1880. He visited the settlement as he usually did, both spring and fall. I heard him mention Eyvindur when he was talking to one of the farmers and it was clear that he had great affection for my friend. I remember clearly what he said.

"Eyvindur Atli is a fine young man. If you do anything for him, he does more than just thank you with words."

When I arrived in Winnipeg in 1882, Eyvindur had left to go to the United States.

SIGHVATUR

I n my essays about Icelandic settlers in Nova Scotia I have often referred to the time when I was an errand boy in a gold mine on the Atlantic coast. That was in the summer of 1880, and I was fourteen years old. I had board and room with six Icelandic men who were regular workers in the mine. Their shanty stood beside a shelter-belt of ever-green trees just north of the town. We were close to the main road, which passed through the Mooseland Hills and con-tinued eastward to the ocean. Several people from the Icelandic community in Mooseland came to call on us there. One of our visitors was a man named Sighvatur. I never heard his father's name because he had adopted the surname Sutherland.

Sighvatur knew all six miners very well. Indeed, one of them was a close relative. They had all travelled together from Iceland to Ontario in 1874. All seven returned to the Maritimes later that fall. Sighvatur left the group in New Brunswick and subsequently tried various jobs in Halifax, Lockeport and other places along the Atlantic coast while his friends elected to stay at the gold mine in Nova Scotia. This time Sighvatur came from Newfoundland. He had been working in a copper mine there for three or four years. He came to visit his friends once more before leaving to join his brother, who had moved to Boston the previous year. I remember Sighvatur's visit very well.

He was a man in his early thirties, of barely average height. He had dark hair, quick eyes and a forthright manner. I heard the miners say that he was conscientious, hard-working and honest. He had his own opinions, they said, and, if he took a stand on any issue, he could not be budged. He arrived on a Saturday evening in early August of 1880, and he stayed until Monday morning. That was the only time I saw him. He told us stories about some of his experiences, and I remember one of them particularly well. This is the story that Sighvatur told.

While I was knocking back and forth along the Atlantic coast during the summer of 1875, by sheer luck I found work with a certain wholesale company. This was in a fairly large port city and the company had three large warehouses. The manager of the company was a chap named Milman. He was an older man by this time, said to be rather demanding of his employees and hard to please but reliable in his business dealings. As soon as I started to speak, he realized that English was not my first language. Right away, he wanted to know about my nationality. When I told him that I was Icelandic, he found that hard to believe. "I have never met an Icelandic person," he said. "I have met Norwegians, Swedes and Danes, and you probably resemble some of them, or you might resemble some people from Northern Ireland."

"Nevertheless, I am Icelandic," I said. "I was born and raised in Iceland."

"All right, then, if you say so," said Milman. He had

nearly thirty men in his employ and some had worked for him for many years. I understood that everyone liked to work there and they felt that their wages were reasonable. I was there for almost two years and, all that time, the same men remained on the job except for the night watchman. It seemed that, for some reason, the watchman was changed every two or three months. The watchman who was there when I started left after about a month and he never came back to that neighbourhood. The next watchman was there less than three months and he was asked to leave. He was never seen around there again. I never heard anyone say why these men were dismissed. It was as if no one thought there was anything unusual about that. I got the idea that this job, watchman at Milman's warehouses, was not as straightforward as one might think.

Because I had had reason to expect that I would have a permanent job there, I built myself a log cabin that was both near the warehouses and near the ocean. I had permission from Milman to put up my cabin there because the company owned that strip of land. I bought myself a stove, a small table, two chairs and a couch. I found that this arrangement would be much cheaper for me than paying for board and room in the town. Then, one day in the spring of 1877, Milman mentioned to me that he would like me to take on the job of night watchman.

"Tomorrow I will dismiss the man who has been watchman for the past two months," he said. "He is a good man but he is not quite up to the job. I think that you, on the other hand, have most of the qualities that are called for in a good watchman. I would like you to start tomorrow night and, if you like the work and the company is pleased with

the way you do things, you can stay on and I will raise your wages for the following month. You will be on duty at the warehouses from the time that the workmen leave at night until they start the next morning. You can go home at midnight to have a meal but remember to be back here within the hour. Tomorrow night I will give you further details."

I told Mr. Milman that I would undertake this job, since he seemed anxious for me to try it. However, I really was not very pleased because I felt sure that he would release me from my job in one month's time. The following evening I started my new position after Mr. Milman had carefully explained my duties. Then, one night at the beginning of the fourth week that I was on the watch, I went to my cabin at midnight as usual to get myself some tea and a bite to eat. I had just put some bread and syrup on the table and made the tea when I heard heavy footsteps outside the cabin. I waited to see whether someone would knock at the door. No one knocked. A few moments passed and then, suddenly, the door was opened roughly and in walked a big man, both tall and heavyset. He stopped near the table. I thought he might be about twenty-five years old. He was rather good-looking but his face was dark and dirty as if he had been working in a coal mine. His hands looked fairly clean and white. He was wearing an old cloak that was quite long and he had worn, muddy-looking shoes on his feet. On his head, he wore an old, grey hat. He did not address me at all and did not seem to pay any attention to me, but he moved up to the table and looked at the food as if he would like to help himself to it.

I said quickly, "Who are you? Where have you come

from? What is your business here?"

He seemed startled, looked at me and said, "I am a wanderer and I come from all directions, like the wind. I came from the north yesterday, from the south this morning and I'll be going west in the next few days. I came here to see how hospitable you are. I am very hungry and I would appreciate any courtesy you could show me.

"Sit at the table and help yourself to the food I have there," I offered.

He sat down at the table right away. "Where is the cream for the tea?" he asked.

"I never take cream in my tea," I replied.

"Where is the sugar?"

"I never buy sugar," I said, "but I put syrup in my tea. There is a can of syrup on the table. Help yourself."

He put two or three teaspoons of syrup into the tea, stirred it well and tasted it. "It doesn't taste too bad. A person could drink this," he said, "but you have forgotten to put butter on the table."

"I never buy butter," I said. "Instead, I put syrup on my bread."

He took a slice of bread and put syrup on it. When he had eaten three big slices of bread, all that was on the table, and he had drunk all the tea, he passed the cup to me and asked whether there might be a little more in the teapot.

"The teapot is empty," I said, "and I do not have time to make more because I am a night watchman. I have to be back on the job in ten minutes. I must ask you to leave now. Goodnight."

"How long is it till day?" he asked.

"It is almost one hour after midnight."

"Listen to what I have to say," he said. "I usually stay up during the night and rest during the day. I will take the watch for you. I can see that you are tired. Stretch out on the couch there and have a rest. Just tell me where I have to go and I will watch for you and then I will wake you up at dawn. In this way, I will repay the hospitality you have shown me. How about it?"

"No," I said. "I cannot have you do my work for me. Goodnight."

I blew out the lamp and opened the door and we both stepped outside. I locked the door with a key and started out for the warehouses. The visitor went off in another direction without any goodbyes. He seemed irked because I did not accept his offer.

The following night I drank my tea and ate my bread without interruption in the cabin. Just as I was going to put out the light and go back to work, the door was pushed open and in walked the same man who had visited me the night before.

"What is the matter now?" I asked. "Are you hungry or what?"

"Oh no," he said. "I am not hungry now. I met some good people who offered me both food and drink, and the waiter at the hotel by the sea offered me this when I arrived there this morning."

He pulled a little flask from his pocket.

"This is first-rate French cognac. I never drink alcoholic beverages so I thought I would ask you to accept it. You need something to give you strength through the night and you can sip now and again while you are working."

"*No, thank you,*" *I said.* "*I am like you. I never taste alcoholic drinks.*"

"*That is unusual,*" *he said.*

"*And I will tell you something else,*" *I said.* "*And that is that, even if I drank and I owned a bottle full of the finest cognac, I would not be taking a drop of it tonight, for good reason.*"

"*Strange,*" *said my visitor.*

I looked at my watch.

"*Now I have to leave,*" *I said, and I blew out the lamp. I walked out of the cabin and the fellow followed me out, flask in hand.*

"*You're in a big hurry,*" *he said.*

"*Goodnight,*" *I said, as I locked the door and headed towards the warehouses.*

The man stood beside the door and called after me, "*How long is it until day?*"

"*The time is almost one hour after midnight,*" *I told him.*

The next night I did not go to the cabin to avoid another encounter with the tramp. I carried with me a couple of slices of bread and a bottle of tea. At two in the morning, I had to go to another building. It was routine for me to open certain windows and close some others throughout the night. When I was opening the side door into the building, I was aware of a big man standing nearby. Although it was quite dark, I realized right away that here was the same man who had let himself into my cabin on the two previous nights. At this point, I suspected that this man was no ordinary tramp.

"*Who is there?*" *I asked.*

"Your friend," was the answer, and the man came right up to the door of the warehouse, which was half open by now.

"No further," I said. "What are you wanting?"

"I would like to spend the rest of the night chatting with you to help you spend the time and, in that way, I can thank you for the friendship you have shown to a poor stranger."

"You have to leave here at once," I commanded, "because I am going into the warehouse and I will be busy there until dawn."

"I am going to come in whether you like it or not," he said.

"I say that you are not going into this building," I said.

"You cannot prevent me. I am bigger and stronger than you are."

As he said this, he grabbed my shoulder and tried to push me out of the doorway. I resisted although I knew right away that he was very strong and I was a lightweight in his hands. Just as he swung me away from the door, almost by accident, I put my foot in front of him and he fell and lost his grip on me. It took him a moment to get up and I knew he had hurt himself.

"I hope you are not hurt too badly," I said, as I shut the door to the warehouse, "but remember that this was your own fault. Get up! Go away! Don't come back here ever again!"

He stood up, looked at me a moment and said, "Tell me one thing. How long is it till day?"

"I can't see my watch in the darkness," I said. "It is not my job to tell people what time it is. My job is to watch

here at night so that no tramps or criminals break into these warehouses. Go away from here at once!"

I said this knowing full well that I was no match for him and I knew that this fellow could fight me off at any time. He had the strength of three men of my size.

"Since that is the kind of person you are, I guess we had better part for now," he said.

"Yes," I said. "Go away and stay away."

He left at that point.

The following night I went back to my cabin around midnight and drank my tea in peace. I was not disturbed that night, either at the cabin or at the warehouses. This was a Thursday morning. Four nights passed and everything was quiet. The next Monday morning I was about to leave my shift as the workmen returned for the day. One of the men stopped to give me a message from Mr. Milman. I was to go to the office to see him at nine o'clock in the morning. I was sure that he was going to dismiss me.

At nine o'clock, I walked over to the office. As it happened, Mr. Milman was not there. He was talking to a man in the next room but one of the office clerks told me that he would be free in a few minutes and I should sit down and wait for him. I had just sat down when I noticed a young man, big and strong-looking and well-dressed. He was sitting at a desk in one corner of the office and he was looking over some documents. I was taken aback because I realized right away that this was the same man who had three times confronted me at midnight. When he was aware that I was staring at him, he nodded his head. I pretended that I had not noticed him. All of a sudden, he stood up, took the papers off his desk and passed them to *another man whose desk was nearby. As he walked past me, he bent down and said, "You likely know me. I have visited you three times and I owe you my gratitude for your good reception."*

"There is no need to thank me for anything," I said.

He walked to the door, looked at me briefly, and left. I approached a clerk and asked him who the young man was.

"He is Mr. Milman's stepson. He has just come home from a long journey through Scandinavia."

Soon after that, Mr. Milman came into the office, greeted me warmly, and asked me to join him in the next room because he wanted to have a few words with me. We moved into the boardroom where he usually received business partners of the wholesale company.

"Now you have been watchman for us for a whole month," said Mr. Milman, when we were seated, "and I can tell you that I want you to continue at that post for some time. I am going to raise your pay by $1.75 per week. My stepson thinks that you are a trustworthy watchman and he believes that your wages should be raised."

"I can tell you one thing, Mr. Milman," I said. "During the past ten minutes, I have come to the decision that it would be best for me to give up this job as watchman right away. I am resigning from this position as of this moment and I will not expect more pay for this past month than was agreed upon at the outset. I hope you understand, although I find it hard to put into words in English that our business is finished."

"What is the reason for this?" asked Mr. Milman, obviously surprised. "Why do you want to leave this job when you have been praised for your performance and you have

been offered a raise?"

"Your stepson knows the reason," I said.

"Surely he is not the reason for your resignation?" said Mr. Milman. "He has assured me that you have all the qualities that one would look for in a good watchman. You do not sleep when you are on the watch, you do not drink, and you do not allow anyone to accompany you in the warehouses at night."

"And how could he know that?" I asked.

"He has ways to find these things out."

"Yes, I am sure," I said. "But he did that in a way I did not like."

"Don't fuss; he had unusual methods of checking your loyalty and your honesty as watchman. You are a foreigner. You say you are Icelandic. There is no one here who can vouch for you. No one knows you or any other Icelandic people. I had to be assured that you would be fit for the work that I assigned you. My stepson offered to sound you out and he is pleased with the results of his test."

"However that may be," I said, " I have definitely decided to quit the job and leave here for good."

"Well and good," said Mr. Milman. "I do not want to keep anyone here against his will. But I'll tell you one thing, you will have to continue as watchman for at least two weeks, according to company rules, so that I will have time to find someone to replace you."

"I understand," I said, and I took my leave and made my way to my cabin. I worked for two weeks. When I called at the office to pick up my wages and to drop off the keys and the lantern, Mr. Milman asked me once again

whether I was still determined to leave. I said that was so.

"I am not happy to see you go," he said, and he shook my hand. "But I wish you the best of luck. Farewell."

A few days later I sold my cabin, my stove, my couch and chairs at reasonably good prices. Mr. Milman was the one who found a buyer for me. Soon after that, I moved to Newfoundland and found work in the copper mine.

This is the story that Sighvatur told the Icelandic miners in Nova Scotia in August of 1880.

BESSI

In 1880, at the age of fourteen, I had board and room with some Icelandic men who lived in a little shanty that stood beside a grove of evergreens high up on a hillside north of a mining town in Nova Scotia.

There were six men there, all working in the gold mine, and the one who seemed to be their spokesman was Jón Jónsson. He was the oldest one of the group, an energetic man and a good fellow altogether. On summer evenings when the weather was fine we often sat on the south side of the house to relax. Sometimes one of the men read out loud to entertain us.

One Sunday evening in early August, we noticed a man with a pack on his back. He was coming along the road that led through the town and he stopped to talk to a group of boys. One of the boys pointed in our direction, and the traveller soon turned up the path, which wound up the hillside to our shanty.

"This is definitely an Icelander," said one of the miners. "That looks like a *koffort* that he is carrying on his back. We are going to have a good visitor."

His guess was right. An Icelandic man came up the hill. He was dressed in brown Icelandic homespun clothes and he carried a small Icelandic chest on his back. He was of average height and well-proportioned. When he came closer we saw that he was a young man, probably less than twenty years old. He was fair complexioned, rather good-looking, and he had a kindly and intelligent look about him.

"Are you Icelandic?" he asked as he approached. He seemed rather shy.

Jón spoke up and said yes, indeed, we were all Icelandic. The visitor was obviously relieved. Right away he set the chest down, took off his hat and walked around to shake hands with each of us. He said his name was Bessi and he told us his father's name, but I have since forgotten that. He had just arrived from Iceland but he had rested for a few days in the settlement in Mooseland Hills. One of the farmers there had given him a letter addressed to Jón Jónsson. In the letter he asked Jón to help this young man and to try to find work for him at the coast.

Bessi was received very well by all the miners, just as if he was a relative, and he was made welcome in the house there. Jón said that he would do his best to find some suitable employment for him in the town. That evening Bessi was happy and talkative. He brought news from Iceland, seemed quite well-informed and was interesting to listen to. Of course he stayed with us for the night.

The next morning when the miners went to work, Bessi went with them. Jón talked to his foreman and asked whether he could find some work for this young man. The answer was that there was no work for him there. In fact, there were more men than they needed in the mine just then. Later on there would be more work to do and then he could apply again if he so wished. "But I'll tell you another thing," said the foreman to Jón, "I am sure that my cousin, Harrigan, would be glad to have this young man with him this fall. He has a piece of land close to town, and he wants to do some clearing so that he can plough it up and grow some oats and buckwheat next spring. The land there is stony, and here and there it is covered with brush. There is lots of work to do there. My cousin, I have to say, is a bit lazy. Shall I say, he likes his rest and comfort? He doesn't get much done on the land unless he has someone to work with him and keep him at it. I'll talk to him today and find out whether he would like to give your friend a job."

Jón was pleased with this because he had met Harrigan and he said he was sure that Bessi would accept the job. He had felt badly when there was no work for him in the mine.

Two days later Harrigan came for Bessi. He arrived in a two-wheeled cart pulled by a bay horse. Harrigan was a big, handsome man with black hair and large, dark eyes. He was probably about thirty years old, quiet and courteous in manner, and he spoke slowly and in rather a low voice. His home was about two miles from the town and his house was sheltered by a high hill near the seaside. Nearby there was a long pier and a large boathouse. The strip of land that Harrigan owned stretched all the way from the ocean to the top of the hill. It was about one-half mile in length and about a quarter of a mile in width.

Harrigan had the idea that there might be gold in this strip of land, particularly in the hill itself. He had done some digging in a few different places but to no avail. Men called him Harrigan the Prospector when they talked about him between themselves. He had a good reputation and he was generally well liked, but he was known to be a little bit eccentric and cranky at times. He was Irish and his wife was

Scottish. They had a son who was five years old, a beautiful little boy. He was a much-loved only child.

Harrigan said that he had plenty of work for Bessi to do until Christmastime and he offered twelve dollars per month along with board and room. He said that he hoped that the two of them would get along well, but he was sorry that Bessi knew very little English.

Bessi picked up his chest and prepared to leave with Mr. Harrigan. When he said goodbye to us, he said that he would like to look in and see us on Sundays.

Next Saturday evening, Harrigan came around and stopped with us for a short while. Jón offered him a seat. "How do you like the new hired man?" he asked.

"I came here especially to have a word with you about him," said Harrigan. "I have a little complaint about him."

"Does he not work hard enough? Or does he not do good work? Or what is the problem?"

"I have no complaints about him as a workman," said Harrigan. "He is very hard-working. He keeps on working almost as if he cannot stop himself. He has been picking rocks from the hillside north of the house for the past two days, and I have seldom seen anyone work so hard. But it seems as if he expects that I should be with him all the time and work like he does and be prepared to help him loosen the largest rocks, roll them out and lift them onto the rock piles. It seems that he cannot bear to see me stand or sit idly by. 'Work, work!' he says over and over if I come and stand beside him to tell him what I want him to do. Of course I do not understand him entirely and I am sure he has trouble understanding what I am saying to him. That is to be expected since he is a newcomer in this country. I would not blame him if he had some shortcomings, but I do not like him to tell me what to do. Now I want you to tell him when he comes here next that it is not customary in this country that the servant gives orders to his employer, and he should not be surprised even if I do not work along with him all the time."

Jón promised to discuss this with Bessi but he said he was sure that Mr. Harrigan misunderstood his workman as far as this was concerned. Harrigan said that it was possible that he misunderstood, but he still wanted Jón to mention this problem in conversation with Bessi. They left matters like that for the time being.

The next day Bessi came to visit us. He seemed happy and well. We asked how he liked his job.

"Oh, I am happy about everything," he answered, "Mr. Harrigan is a good employer. He and his wife are kind to me and the little boy is a joy. I have good food, a good bed and a room all to myself."

"Mr. Harrigan says that you are hard-working and that you do the work well, but that he finds it hard to understand you. He feels that you always want him to work along with you. He cannot do that all the time because he has other things to attend to."

"It is all right with me even though I work alone," said Bessi, "but I am always glad when he comes with me, especially if he helps me lift the biggest rocks. He never gets tired of talking to me and I am grateful for that. Of course I do not understand much of what he says to me." Bessi spent some time with us and said that he would be back the following weekend.

A few evenings later Harrigan came again to see us. He

seemed rather upset. We offered him a seat. "Well, how are things going now?" one of the men asked.

"It gets worse," said Harrigan. He took his pipe from his pocket, filled it with tobacco and started to smoke. "I almost feel like letting him go. He irritates me in many ways."

"Is he getting lazy or careless about his work?" asked Jón.

"No, far from it," said Harrigan, and pulled at his pipe. "He is most willing and a very good workman. In fact, he seems to work harder and harder every day. He digs stones out of the ground, rolls big rocks down the slope and gathers them into huge piles. He is always good-natured as can be. He is happy and full of energy and he is particularly good to my boy. But he doesn't know how to use an axe, he can't milk the cows and he feeds the horse way more cornmeal than is necessary. The other thing is that whenever I come to see him when he is working, he always suggests somehow that he expects me to start working with him. That doesn't bother me so much nowadays because I am getting used to that. There is another thing that bothers me more and that I will not be able to put up with for any length of time. He has started getting up before dawn or as soon as the sun comes up, and right away he starts working with the rocks or cutting firewood. He always moves quietly when he gets up, walks slowly across the floor and closes the doors carefully. Still, I always wake up as soon as he leaves the house. I have tried again and again to make him understand that this is not the right time to be getting up in my house, and he must not be getting up so early so long as I am his employer. I guess he has not understood me and I would like you to explain to him how I feel about this." The men promised to go over this with Bessi and that made Harrigan look happier. Shortly afterwards, he walked to town to meet some of his relatives there.

Fairly early the next Sunday, Bessi came to see us. He was as cheerful as could be. He spent most of the day with us, but just before he left Jón asked him whether he was still happy with his job.

"I like it better and better," said Bessi. "Mr. Harrigan is very good to me and I am starting to understand some of the things he says to me. He has taught me how to use an axe, how to harness the horse and how to milk the cows, and he has taught me other things that I didn't know how to do before. Once I went with him on a boat out to an island far out in the bay. He said then that he could see that I knew how to handle the oars. On the way home we raised a sail and I steered. Mr. Harrigan thought that I handled the boat well. I like best the times when he works with me."

"But he thinks that you get up way too early," said Jón. "He wakes up as soon as you stir and he asked me to tell you that."

"That is true," said Bessi, smiling. "I sometimes get up early because I do not sleep well and I don't like to lie in bed after I wake up. I am homesick at times and I am wakeful at night. The homesickness disappears when I start working. I am sure that Mr. Harrigan doesn't blame me, though I am awake both early and late." Bessi left us and went back to his boarding place.

The next Saturday night Mr. Harrigan came again just as we were getting up from the supper table. He was obviously unhappy. He sat down beside the stove, took his pipe out of his pocket, brought out his tobacco and began to smoke.

"Now you have news for us?" asked Jón.

"I just came to let you know that I am about to dismiss the

young fellow because he is getting too big for my liking, and in fact he has been that way from the beginning. I only took him as my hired man because your foreman, my cousin, begged me to."

"Is he slowing down? Has he been neglecting his work?" asked Jón.

"Far from it," said Harrigan, and he puffed away at his pipe. "He always works like crazy and he is a good servant.

"Has he learned to use an axe?"

"Yes, he has learned that and he would make a good lumberjack," said Harrigan.

"Has he learned to milk the cows?"

"Yes, it did not take him long to learn that, and he drives the cows to pasture in the mornings and brings them home in time at night. He is also quick to do chores around the house. He takes out the ashes from the stove and he carries the water from the well. He cuts firewood and brings it in and he is helpful with other jobs as well."

"Does he still give the horse too much cornmeal?"

"He takes good care of the horse and he no longer feeds him too much."

"Does he still get up too early?"

"Nowadays he gets up at the same time as I get up myself," said Harrigan.

"So why do you feel that you have to fire the young man?" asked Jón. "What has he done wrong?"

"I'll tell you," said Harrigan, speaking very slowly. "He is putting himself on an equal footing with me, or in other words his attitude toward me does not please me. It seems to me that he always forgets that I, as his employer, am not his fellow worker or his pal."

"In what way does he step out of line?"

"In many ways. He has for example given me a push when I have been checking to see what he was working at. And just yesterday I helped him lift out a very big stone. Then he hit me across the shoulders so hard that it hurt. I suppose he did that in fun but I do not care for that kind of joking around from anyone—least of all from my hired man, whom I hardly know and who can only speak a few words in a language that I understand. I have therefore decided that I will have the fellow leave next Monday morning. I will give him his full pay and will bring him to town. I know that he will come here tomorrow, so you can tell him this."

"We will explain all this to him," said Jón. "You may bring him and his chest here on Monday. He can have board and room with us and we will try to get work for him with our foreman, your cousin, at the mine."

"Have it your way," said Harrigan.

Bessi came to see us early on Sunday morning. He was cheerful as usual. Jón told him what Harrigan had said to us, that he would lose his job the next day and that he would be moving in with us.

"Mr. Harrigan must have been joking when he said that I hit him on the shoulder," said Bessi smiling, "but the other day we were rolling some stones onto the slope and he was sometimes in my way because he moves slowly. I often had to warn him and one time I pushed him so he would not be in front of the stone I was about to roll over the edge. The day before yesterday he came to me when I was struggling to get a very large stone out of the ground just in front of the house. He started helping me right away and we soon loosened the stone. Then I realized that he is very strong because he easily lifted the stone and carried it a short distance. When that job was done I slapped him on the shoulders in friendly fashion and I said to him in Icelandic, 'You have strength in those fingers, Mr. Harrigan!' I can't believe that he wants to fire me for these reasons, but of course I am ready to leave whenever he says. I am prepared for whatever happens."

No more was said. Just after lunch Bessi left to go back to Harrigan's. We were expecting to see him at our house the next day, but early on Monday morning when the miners were getting ready to leave for work we saw Harrigan striding up the hill. There was no sign of Bessi and his chest. Jón walked out to meet Harrigan and enquired after Bessi.

"The young man is with me," Harrigan said, happily, "and I came to let you know that you don't have to bother about finding work for him in the mine, because he will work for me all winter, and I have raised his wages so he is very pleased."

"But on Saturday night you told us that you were going to dismiss him today because he was getting too close to you," said Jón.

"Everything has changed for the better," said Harrigan. "We had a long talk last night and I understood him completely and he understood me, although he doesn't know much English. I owe him a great deal because of something he did for me. My wife and I consider him our good friend and my little boy loves him. The young man asked me to give you his regards and to tell you that he will not be visiting you next Sunday. Have a good day!"

Having said this, he started off for home and walked at a good pace. He never came back to see us after that.

The Icelandic miners thought it more than a little strange that Mr. Harrigan should change his mind overnight. It was difficult to guess what the reason could be. Some wondered if Harrigan and Bessi had stumbled on gold when they were digging in the slope north of the house, but that was not the case. The following Sunday, two of the miners went to Harrigan's home to see Bessi. Mr. and Mrs. Harrigan received them well and Bessi was in good form. The miners asked him whether he knew why Harrigan had not fired him on Monday morning as he had planned. Bessi answered this way: "Things happened in such a way that Harrigan all of a sudden changed his mind on Sunday night." He did not want to say any more about it.

Bessi seldom visited us after that. He stayed with the Harrigans and he was still there when I left Nova Scotia in 1882. It was said in the neighbourhood that, through quick action and presence of mind, Bessi had managed to save the little boy when he fell off the pier in the fall of 1880.

BOY BURNS

For eight months in 1880, I boarded with the Icelandic miners who worked for the well-respected Daniel Hoss in Tangier, Nova Scotia. The house we lived in was quite low, fairly long and built from rough lumber with tar paper on the outside. On the side that faced the town there was a door and a large window. There were also windows on each end of the house, but none on the side that faced the trees. The house was divided in the middle into two rooms. In one room there was the stove, a long table, two benches—one on each side of the table—some cooking utensils, a few dishes and so on. The other room was used as sleeping quarters. In it were a few Icelandic chests and some simple bedclothes. The miners slept on the floor on straw mattresses or sometimes on mattresses filled with soft evergreen branches.

There were six Icelandic miners living in the house while I was there, and Jón Jónsson seemed to be in charge. He was the eldest of the group, a man known for his determination and hard work. The men were all reliable, intelligent and generous. They were all very good and kind to me, and I felt very content while I was with them. They did not have much free time because they worked ten hours or more every single workday. They cooked morning and evening, swept the floor every day and cleaned every Saturday evening. They washed their own clothes and did their own mending. But they never baked bread. Their bread was baked for them in a house in the town.

In spite of all the work they had to do, they still took time for a little fun, especially on Sundays. They also had a few Icelandic books, which they read when time allowed. I remember that they had a book of Scandinavian myths, some of the sagas, *The Iliad* in free verse as translated by Sveinbjörn Egilsson, and *Folk Stories* by Jón Arnason. One of the youngest miners often read out loud for us from these books, and he read so well and with such good delivery that it was a joy to listen to him. He was barely twenty years old but he was a big man, dignified in appearance and handsome. He was outstanding among all the young workers at the mine.

I remember many incidents from the time that I spent in Tangier. I particularly remember an interesting man who visited us one Sunday morning in late May of 1880. I remember also a strange happening that occurred the night before he came. It had nothing to do with his visit, but I'll still tell the story in just a few words.

It was late on Saturday, when we were about to take our rest, that we heard some small stones banging down on the roof. It was obvious that the stones came from the north because nothing was heard except on the roof and on the wall that faced the grove of evergreens. After this noise had continued for a little while, the men went out to look around. As soon as they came outside the onslaught stopped. It was a cloudy evening, and by this time it was dark. There was no wind. There was no evidence of anyone around.

After waiting for a few moments, the men went back into the house. In just a few moments, stones and gravel were showered on the roof even more forcefully than before. The men went back out to investigate. The hail of stones stopped. We walked all around the house and followed the row of trees, back and forth. Nothing unusual was noticed. No sooner had we entered the house than the same attack started all over again. This continued until midnight, stones falling on the roof when we were inside but stopping as soon as we came out. This happened six or seven times, and then one of the men suggested that they take the old shotgun that they had hanging on the wall, fill it with powder but no shells and shoot into the air in front of the house. All agreed that this would be worth trying, so the shotgun was quickly loaded with powder and a shot was fired just outside the door. The rain of gravel on the roof stopped immediately and that was the end of that. That was the only time in the six years that the Icelanders worked in Tangier that anything like that happened. We never knew who the pranksters were. Some said, jokingly of course, that this was a foreboding of the visit from the stranger who called on us the following morning. Now we will turn our attention to that visitor and his reason for coming to see us.

On Sunday morning at about nine o'clock we noticed a man coming up the path that led from the town and up the hillside to our house. We watched him from the window. He walked slowly, stopped every once in a while and turned around with his hands on his hips to look over to the town as if he were admiring the beautiful view. As he approached the house he took off his hat and fixed his hair. He was rather good-looking, about thirty years old, dark-haired and clean-shaven. He wore a grey suit, which fitted him nicely, and he had a fine, white scarf, which was carefully tied. He looked every inch a gentleman, but we thought there was an air of mystery about him. The men were sure they had never seen this man before and they wondered what business he could have with them.

As soon as he came up to the house he knocked at the door, rather hesitantly as if he was unsure of himself. When the door was opened, he stepped inside without waiting to be invited. He wished us good morning politely, laid his hat on the table and sat down on the bench that faced the door. The men received his greeting cheerfully and made him welcome.

"I believe that you are Icelanders," he said, after he had looked us over for a moment. He said that slowly and in a low voice. I thought that his eyes were serious, and he looked as if he had not slept well that night.

The men replied, "Yes, we are all Icelanders, through and through."

"Six men and one boy," noted the visitor.

"Yes," said one of the miners, "there are seven of us, of good Icelandic stock."

"I don't doubt that," said the visitor, and smiled at us, "and are there other Icelanders in this town?" He was told that we were the only Icelanders in Tangier. He did not seem convinced. He waited a moment and frowned a little bit.

"I have an important errand here," he said. "I will tell you who I am. My name is Mann, Ernest Mann, and I live in Halifax. I am a baker, but I have sometimes had to take other work. I have had many irons in the fire. I came here yesterday morning on the ship that is docked here in the harbour.

This evening I will board the ship again and sail back overnight. But I repeat, I have urgent business with you Icelanders." He laid one hand on the table as he said this, and I noticed that his hand was white and thin.

One of the miners said that he was welcome to discuss with them but added, as a joke, that none of them was a baker. "I am not looking for a baker," said Mr. Mann, "but I am making inquiries about a certain man who is Icelandic. I got to know him a little last year, but the last time I saw him was on New Year's Eve in Halifax. I need to find this man. I was told that when he left Halifax he went straight to Tangier and that he lives here, so I have come to you to get information about him."

The miners asked the name of the man he was looking for.

"His name is Burns, Boy Burns," said Mr. Mann.

"That is not an Icelandic name," said one of our men.

"He is definitely an Icelander," said Mr. Mann. "I heard him more than once say that he was born and brought up in Iceland, and that he had recently come to this country. I was with him for almost half a year and he had great difficulty speaking English. I know that he wrote letters to a woman in Iceland because I mailed two of them for him. He always said that his name was Boy Burns, how he spelt that I do not know. Those of us who were with him last fall always called him Boy, and spelt that B-O-Y."

The miners said that neither name was Icelandic.

"Are there some Icelandic names that are similar?" asked Mr. Mann. The men said that the names Bogi and Bjorn were similar, and that it was possible that the man's name was Bogi Björnsson, but they had not heard that any Icelander by that name had come to America.

"Likely he changed his name after he came to America," said Mr. Mann, in a low voice.

"Has this man done anything wrong?" asked one of the miners.

"That is a matter of opinion," said Mr. Mann, sighing, "but, so that you know how important it is for me to find Boy Burns, I will tell you a short story if you are willing to listen." We all indicated that we were anxious to hear the story he had to tell.

The story took place near the Strait of Canso not so far from here. There is a town called Port Mulgrave, and nearby are large gypsum and limestone quarries. You have likely heard about Mr. Cormigan, the limestone king. He has one foot in Halifax and the other in Port Mulgrave. He owns a huge limestone quarry on the west side of the strait, near Port Mulgrave, and he employs many men. I was one of his employees last year. Around the middle of the summer Mr. Cormigan went to Halifax for a few days. When he returned he brought with him a young man, rather small, with fair hair and steel-grey eyes. He was said to be an Icelander, just arrived from Iceland. He was called Boy Burns. He pronounced his name like that himself. He knew only a few words in English when he came to Port Mulgrave, and those few words he spoke with a strong foreign accent. Mr. Cormigan said that a friend of his in Halifax had asked him to look after this Icelander, and he said that he was going to give him work in the quarry at least until Christmas. "Be good to the boy, lads," he said to his workmen, "for he is a youth on his own and far from home."

Boy Burns started work in the quarry and proved to be a good worker. He was energetic even though he was small, he was nimble as a cat and he had more stamina than anyone else in the crew did. He was cheerful, laughed easily and was obviously a bit of a joker. I never saw him shirk away from anything and he seemed to have good self-control. He tried hard to learn English but he found it difficult. His accent sounded strange and his sentences always seemed to have the words in the wrong order. Usually, though, we could follow what he was trying to say. We called him Boy and we all liked him except for one person, our foreman, Ben Killam. From the first day that Boy came to work there, Killam never gave him a chance. He seemed from the beginning to take a strong dislike to this ever-cheerful, innocent-looking foreigner. He always talked harshly to him or jeered at him. Even when we sat at table he had to criticize Boy and ridicule him and his countrymen at every turn. Once he said to me, "I am sure that old Cormigan has brought this barbarian here just to irritate me." Sometimes he suggested that Cormigan had Boy there as a spy so he could tell him what the workers said about him (Cormigan) between themselves. Many times Killam said that either one, he or Boy, would have to leave before the year was over. In short, it seemed that it was an intolerable imposition that he should have to deal with the young man. For a long time Mr. Cormigan did not know anything about the foreman's attitude towards Boy because he lived in Port Mulgrave and only came out to the workplace once in a while, for two or three hours at a time.

Now, make a note of this! Near the quarry where we

worked there was little log cabin, dug halfway into the ground. In that cabin were stored all kinds of materials that were used for blasting bedrock. The door on the cabin was mounted with iron and had a solid lock. No one ever went into the cabin except the man who was in charge of the blasting operations. He always made sure that the door was locked. However, one evening last fall, just as the miners were going home from work, the log cabin exploded. It seemed very odd because there was no fire nearby and the cabin had not been opened that day. As you can imagine, the accident shocked all the workers. Ben Killam was beside himself with rage. He rushed around swearing and shouting so loud that all who heard him were disgusted. He said that there was no doubt about who had committed this crime. It must have been Boy. Boy and no one else was responsible for the explosion! He had long suspected that this barbarian would cause trouble. Killam rushed at Boy, grabbed him roughly by the shoulder and ordered him to confess his guilt. He said that it was useless for him to deny it because everyone knew that he had been working near the cabin that day.

Boy said that he was innocent. He was calm but serious. He used the few English words he knew to defend himself. All those who had worked with Boy that day said right away that they had never seen him near the cabin and they were sure that he had had nothing to do with the explosion. Killam would not change his mind and said that he did not need any witnesses. He said that he would not stop until Boy had admitted that he had caused the explosion.

The next day Mr. Cormigan came to the mine. He was

told about what had happened the night before, and that Killam blamed Boy. Mr. Cormigan said that he believed that the young man was innocent. What could he gain from destroying the cabin? "He wasn't around when the old storehouse on the hill exploded three years ago," he said quietly to Ben Killam, "and I seem to remember that you told me at that time that rats must have caused the blast." Then Ben Killam finally calmed down a little bit.

"It would be best to drop charges since you, Mr. Cormigan, want to make excuses for this foreigner," he said.

Then Boy spoke in his broken English. We were not able to understand what he said but Mr. Cormigan seemed to understand it right away.

"What is he blathering about?" asked Killam.

"He wants an apology," said Cormigan, "He wants you to ask his forgiveness. I think you should do that," he added.

"No, never," said Killam, and he walked away.

Two or three weeks went by without further trouble. Boy seemed fine; he was cheerful as usual as if nothing had happened. Killam spoke to him with the same harshness as before and ridiculed him as before. No one said one word about the explosion.

One morning Mr. Cormigan came to the workplace and spent some time there. He stayed to have lunch with us at noon. While we sat at the table Boy started talking to Mr. Cormigan and he used a new word that we had never heard from him before. That word was "satisfaction."

"I have to get satisfaction," he said. "Mr. Killam has to let me have satisfaction, he has to ask for forgiveness in

*front of witnesses. Otherwise I will have to go to court to
make things right." We felt that his English had improved
a lot in three weeks.*

*Mr. Cormigan spoke to him very quietly and said that it
would be best to forget this subject altogether. No more
was said that day.*

*The next time Mr. Cormigan stopped to have lunch with
the workmen, Boy said again that he had to have satisfaction from foreman Killam and he mentioned his
forefathers who, as we understood, settled their disputes
with two sharp swords. At first we did not know what he
was talking about, but Mr. Cormigan asked whether he
had in mind to offer Killam to fight a duel. "You have the
old spirit, my lad, but I can tell you that nowadays there is
nothing to be gained from a duel because if one is killed
the other will be hanged. We will just drop this matter and
never mention it again."*

*All of us who heard this talk were surprised that Boy
was so stubborn and that he spoke out in such a way. It
was clear that he was determined to get satisfaction from
Ben Killam, although he did not talk about it to anyone
except Mr. Cormigan.*

*At Christmastime work in the quarry stopped and the
workmen went home. Most lived somewhere near the
Strait of Canso. Boy Burns and I were the only ones who
left by ship. The ship that took us to Halifax left Port
Mulgrave between Christmas and New Year's. Mr.
Cormigan and a few of his men, including Ben Killam,
came with us to the pier. Boy shook hands with everyone
except Ben Killam. At last he walked over to Killam and
said to him in reasonably good English, "Mr. Killam, you*

have done me wrong. I have been falsely accused but I would have forgiven you if you had asked for forgiveness. You have not done that. I would have taken you to court if Mr. Cormigan had not stopped me and I would have taken you on in a fight with a weapon of your choice if that had been possible. You have to make things right."

"Is it money you are after or what?" sneered Killam.

"No," said Boy, "I would hate your money. I give you one chance to ask my forgiveness and I will take your hand and forgive you. Are you ready?" Boy offered his right hand.

"This was well said," said Mr. Cormigan.

Killam did not take the hand that Boy offered. Instead he crossed his arms across his chest and said, "No, and again no. I will never ask forgiveness from an Icelander. Never!"

"As you wish," said Boy, "Then there is only one way left. With all my heart I summon you before the highest court, the judgment of God Himself!" Killam laughed.

Boy went on board ship. On New Year's Eve we arrived in Halifax and I said goodbye to him at the harbour that evening. I have not seen him since.

But this is not the end of the story. Take note of this!

When I came back to Port Mulgrave at Easter, I saw at once that Killam was a changed man. He seemed to be nervous. The summons weighed on his mind like a nightmare, both sleeping and waking, and it hung over his head like a double-edged sword. Now it is his greatest wish that Boy will take back his words and be reconciled with him. He is more than ready to ask his forgiveness in front of witnesses, any number of witnesses. In other words, above all

*he wants the young man to take back his terrible sum-
mons. On behalf of Killam and his relatives I am now
looking for Boy Burns. If I find him and tell him how
things are, I am sure that he will forgive Ben. If I do not
find Boy Burns before long I will have to resort to the so-
called white lie and tell him that I've talked to the young
man and that he has forgiven him.*

"Now that is my story. I hope that you understand why I am
trying so hard to find Boy Burns or whatever his right name
may be," said Mr. Mann.

The Icelandic miners said that they understood the situation but they repeated that they had never heard of this man.
Mr. Mann asked whether it would not be worthwhile to go
to the settlement at Mooseland Hills to find out whether
someone there might know of Boy. We said that he could try
that but we thought it unlikely that that would be of any
help. One of the men asked who had told him that Boy
Burns had left Halifax and gone straight to Tangier to make
his home there. Mr. Mann said that it was the man who
asked Mr. Cormigan to look after Boy in the first place. For
good reasons, the man did not want his name mentioned.

After a short discussion Mr. Mann stood up, shook hands
with each of us, thanked us for our kind reception and said
goodbye. We followed him outside and watched him go
down the path towards the town. He walked slowly. When
he neared the entrance to the mine at the bottom of the hill,
we noticed that he was joined by a man in a long coat and
they walked together toward the ocean.

ABRAHAM BURT

I would like to say a few words about a man I knew briefly when I was a boy in Nova Scotia. His name was Abraham Burt and he died many years ago. All the Icelanders who worked in the gold mine at Tangier, Nova Scotia, between 1875 and 1882 found him helpful and they all thought well of him.

He was an unusual man, rather eccentric in his ways, but always kindly in his dealings and conscientious in his daily work. For the most part, he was quiet and serious. He was a big man but, despite his powerful build, he seemed awkward and his movements seemed stiff and slow. He had a full beard, reddish in colour, and steel-grey eyes that sometimes looked dark and hard. He was said to be Irish and single. He was likely close to fifty years old when I met him in the summer of 1880. At that time, he lived alone in a small log cabin high up in the hillside north of the town of Tangier. He was the closest neighbour to the Icelandic miners. Their shanty stood just a little further east.

Abraham worked for a mine owner named Daniel Hoss. He was an interesting fellow, rather small in stature with a black beard. He was hard-working. He was blustery and loud and he sometimes put his foot in his mouth. Under all the bluster, he was a good sort with a surprisingly tender heart. He employed several Icelanders and he always treated them well and said that they were the best men on the face of the earth, or something to that effect. "The Irish and the Icelanders! They are my men!" said Dan Hoss, and he spoke so loudly that his words echoed through the mine shafts. Hoss was always particularly kind to Abraham Burt. He referred to him as "father," and sought his advice whenever problems arose in the mine. At those times, his tone was low, almost contrite. Although Abraham was slow and stiff, he did his work with care and dedication. He was always the first man to arrive at the mine in the morning and the last to leave at night. Most often his path took him directly from his log cabin in the hillside to the mine and from the mine back to the cabin. Occasionally he might stop at the general store to buy some groceries and other necessities. Rarely did he stop anywhere else, unless he had something out of the ordinary to look after. It was said that he did like a good, stiff drink, but I never saw him with anything of that kind. Indeed, liquor was hard to come by in Tangier in those days except perhaps on special holidays. On the other hand, Abraham would not be without tobacco and he usually walked with a short, black clay pipe stuck in the left side of his mouth.

When the Icelanders came to Tangier, Abraham had already been there for a few years. It was said that he came there from Halifax. In the town, many remarkable stories were told about him; most were likely exaggerated. Many of the stories had to do with dealings between him and Daniel Hoss. It seemed also that, if anything special was said about Hoss, Abraham was likely to be involved in some way.

One of the stories I heard was about the time when

Abraham made Daniel stop gambling with cards. The story I heard went like this:

One winter evening there was great excitement at Daniel Hoss's house. A few friends had met to play a game of poker for money. Abraham was not one of that group. As the evening progressed, it was noticed all of a sudden that there were three aces of hearts in play. No explanation was offered, so silence fell on the group. Hoss suggested that Abraham be asked to come to solve this problem. All agreed to this plan and said they would abide by his decision. Abraham was sent for and he arrived around midnight. It had taken a long time for him to get ready and make his way to the gathering. When he arrived, he sat down at the table without speaking to anyone, lit his pipe, picked up the cards and studied them carefully, frowning the whole time. Then he stood up suddenly, walked to the heater that stood in the middle of the floor, opened it and threw the cards into the fire. He closed the heater carefully and said in a resounding voice, "*Sursum corda!*" Then he walked out of the room without a word. No sooner had he closed the door than the men heard a big bang similar to a shotgun blast and this came from the heater. The men were startled. None of them were Latin scholars but they thought that the words that Abraham spoke at the heater must have had powerful portent.

"This is a wonder!" said Daniel Hoss, at last. "Satan himself must have been here at work! I swear I will not gamble as long as rivers run, grass grows and sun shines."

According to the story, he never touched cards again.

Another story was told about how Daniel Hoss went one New Year's Eve to cheer up Abraham by bringing him a bottle of rum and a gold nugget about the size of a tern's egg.

Hoss returned just before dawn in the arms of Abraham, who had carried him home. Abraham laid him on a couch in the parlour and covered him with a bearskin rug from the floor. Then Abraham patted Hoss in fatherly fashion and said in his deep bass voice, "Sleep well, friend Hoss, in *saecula saeculorum*. Amen."

Yet another story tells how Abraham got all the employers in the gold mine in Tangier to raise the salaries of their workers. The miners there had felt for some time that their wages were low, which was not surprising. Most of them worked ten hours per day for one dollar and twenty-five cents and sometimes even for one dollar. They called a meeting one Saturday night, invited the owners of the mine and asked for a raise. Daniel Hoss spoke for the employers and said that it was outrageous that the men should be asking for higher pay when it was clear that the returns from the mine were such that next to nothing was left after expenses were paid. He finished his talk by saying that no one can get blood from a stone. Then Abraham stood up.

"Friend Hoss," he said, "we workers know that blood cannot be had from a stone, but we know something else. We know that gold can be had from rock. I believe that there is enough gold in your mine that you can well afford to raise our wages. I believe that the vein we found recently is one of the richest that has been found for a long time. I believe your miners are hoping that good gains will be made from that discovery. And I believe…"

Then Daniel Hoss interrupted. "Stop! Stop now, Father Abraham. I know well that your beliefs are strong. They may not move mountains but they can change rock into gold, if it comes to that. Your belief will be rewarded. I promise that I will raise wages for my boys by twenty-five cents per day. And now I don't want to hear any more of this talk." All the other mine owners indicated that they would be willing to follow Hoss's example and adjust their salaries accordingly. The meeting was adjourned and the miners were happy because they knew that Daniel Hoss was as good as his word. They all felt that they had Abraham to thank for the raise, which was not considered little in those days. Abraham won the respect of all concerned and he became a spokesman and advocate for the miners in Tangier.

Most people in Tangier thought that Abraham was a mysterious man and one who should not be crossed. People believed that he had known better days, that he had been well educated, that he had learned other languages and that he had travelled to distant lands. They believed that he had had many adventures in his younger days and had taken risks. For those reasons, they thought, he was now so quiet, so sensible and so settled. In fact, his life story was largely unknown.

Even though he was the closest neighbour to the Icelandic miners, I do not recall that he ever came to our shanty during the eight months that I was there in 1880. Sometimes the men went over to his cabin on Sundays to chat with him. They always felt better after a meeting with Abraham Burt. I respected him and greeted him when I came into the mine in the morning. He seldom returned my greeting, just nodded his head and smiled a little. Shortly before I finished my job at the mine, I had the opportunity to spend some time with him.

It happened one evening in late September of 1880 that Daniel Hoss found that he had to reinforce the landing and the steps into the opening of the mine. He would not entrust this work to anyone but Abraham Burt, and I was asked to be on hand to assist him.

We started around nine o'clock in the evening, working with the aid of a lantern. Abraham worked steadily and, before dawn, the job was almost finished. At that point, he suggested that we should rest for a little while. I was glad to rest because I had been on the run throughout the night. "You must not sleep," said Abraham, as we sat down. He put tobacco into his pipe and started to smoke. He leaned against the wall and crossed his arms over his chest. I was no sooner sitting down than I fell asleep. I woke up because I felt that someone was tickling me under the chin and I laughed. "You were laughing," said Abraham. He sat at arm's length from me.

"Really?" I asked.

"You have to keep awake," he said.

I said, "Yes," but I fell asleep immediately. Then I woke again because I felt that someone tickle me under the chin. I laughed out loud.

"You are laughing," said Abraham. "You must have thought of something funny."

"No," said I. Then I fell asleep for the third time and, once again I woke up, thinking someone was tickling me under the chin. I was laughing louder than before. I looked where Abraham sat and he was smoking quietly with his arms crossed over his chest. I saw his face clearly in the light of the lantern which stood near us. It couldn't have been he who was tickling me under the chin.

"This is strange," he said, quietly. "You were definitely laughing. You must have fallen asleep and you must have dreamed that you saw your girlfriend come riding in a fine carriage pulled by two grey cats. Fourteen-year-old boys often dream such dreams. You must absolutely not fall asleep again."

"How am I going to keep myself awake?" I asked.

"Men often keep themselves awake if they are thinking about something very important," he said.

"What kind of things?" I asked.

"If you think that your life is at risk, you don't fall asleep very quickly," he said. "Think of someone who has upset his boat but has managed to hang on to it and is being tossed around in the waves. He won't get very sleepy. Or if someone clings to a little crag high up in a steep cliff, he won't be sleepy."

"But I am neither out at sea nor high up in a mountain," I said.

"But you could imagine that," said Abraham.

"I can't imagine anything when I am dropping off to sleep," I said.

"One can do everything in imagination," he said. "I'll tell you a short story if you will stay awake and listen. This is the story: Once long ago there was a young man who lived in a little cottage on the west side of a peninsula that stretched far out into the ocean. The coast was rugged and the cliffs went straight down into the sea. On the east side of the peninsula there was a marketplace and the young man often had to go there. To shorten the journey, he sometimes travelled through a narrow pass that led through the cliffs beside the sea. Only experienced mountain climbers took that route. In one spot along the way, there was a ledge that was so narrow that it was impossible to turn around, even if one wanted to.

If you tried to turn, you would lose your balance and fall twenty fathoms or more down the cliff and into the sea. One time when the young man took this path the weather was cold and there was a storm over the ocean. He reached the place that was most dangerous and, just as he was slowly edging around a crag that jutted out of the hillside, he noticed that a man was coming from the other direction. The other man was just about to set his toe on the brink that he himself had to step on to cross the chasm.

"Imagine now that you are the young man, because you can imagine anything. Below you hangs the precipice and the ocean rams the cliffs. It is stormy and cold. You hold with both hands onto a jagged rock that is above you and you touch one foot to a tiny ledge. You cannot go forward because of the man who has met you. You cannot turn around and neither can he. What are you going to do?"

"Are you sleeping again?" he asked

"No," I said. "I am awake."

"Now within a few seconds you have to decide what you should do. One thing is certain. One will have to fall so that the other can save his life. The man who is in your way is your sworn enemy, the only enemy you have. He is the man who has done you all the harm he can possibly do. He has ruined your hopes. He is the man whose wife was once your sweetheart. He is the man who would certainly wish you dead. He is in your way in the narrow pass and his life, like yours, hangs in the balance. Either of you will have to fall. You have to make a decision in the next few seconds which one of you should survive."

"One does not think much in a few seconds," I said.

"You can think through the whole *Book of Job* and the

Lamentations of Jeremiah in just a few seconds when your life is in danger. You are quick to note what terrible risk you face. You are still young and healthy and you would, above all else, like to live a while. You know also that your enemy has a strong wish to live. He will hang on to his grip on the crag as long as possible. He will not give up until he is exhausted. He is young and strong just as you are. He is your equal in determination and endurance. Of course, you could both fall, especially if you make the slightest effort to touch each other. Your enemy will not let go of his grip without seizing you at the same time so that you will follow him over the edge. It would never occur to him to sacrifice himself for you, whom he hates. You are sure of that. But you know that you gain nothing by having him fall with you. You even feel in your heart that you do not wish to see him dead and you would not like to see him fall down the cliff. You know that that would weigh on your conscience for the rest of your life. On the other hand, he would not be conscience-stricken if you fell. He would not blame himself and he would not tell anyone that he had met you in the pass. The secret would never be revealed. No one would ever know in what way you had fallen. Your body might be discovered but no one would know, except your enemy, under what circumstances you lost your life. Now, what are you going to do?"

"I simply don't know," I said.

"You know that either one or the other will have to lose his life. Not both, but either one.

"And you ask yourself, all of a sudden, whether your life is more precious than his life. For yourself, your life is more important, of course. From other points of view, that is not necessarily so. You are a single man, not tied to anyone. You have no close relatives, only a few friends. But your enemy has a good position, many relatives, parents, is married and has two young children.

It is clear that his life is a thousand times more precious than yours is. Then comes the question whether you have any duty to sacrifice your life for his precious life. The answer is this: you owe this man nothing. You wish him no good, but rather the opposite. His parents and his siblings, his cousins and his friends have never shown you anything but contempt. But his wife, young and beautiful and talented, what about her? Does she deserve that you sacrifice your life for the man she loves? Perhaps. Still, you know that between you and her the rift is final even though your mind shrinks from that thought. Then there are this man's children, his two young children. Have you any quarrel with them, the innocents? That is another matter. They will lose the most if their father dies when they are still so young. Do they deserve that you sacrifice your life for them? Your heart is torn. You are faced with the ultimate decision. You have to decide to be one kind of man or another. Are you awake or not?"

"I am awake," I said.

"Now comes something else. You know that it is man's holy duty to fight death till the end. Is it then a question whether one should sacrifice one's life for others? Now you think about the afterlife. You believe that you will have to come before the judgement of your Maker. He is a stern judge but also righteous. What will be His view of it all, if you throw yourself over the edge so that your enemy may live? You think about it and, once again, you face the awful choice. Which kind of man are you? You look at your enemy and you think you see him shudder as he faces death. If you are to give him a chance to save himself, then you must not wait too long to throw yourself down. Are you still undecided?"

"I'll let you decide," I said.

"You do not hesitate any longer. You look at the mountain that towers above you, you look at the sky, you look out to sea and you look down at the surf. You look all around you. You look at everything except your enemy. You close your eyes. You give your spirit into the hands of Him who gave you life. You loosen your grip on the crag and you hurl yourself over the edge. You relive your life, like a dream, in one second. Are you awake or not?"

"I am awake," I said. "Is that the end of the story?"

"Unbelievable as it may seem, the young man was saved. His fall was noticed by crew members on a ship that was resting in a sheltered cove on the east side of the peninsula. The men found him, more dead than alive, brought him on board and revived him."

"What became of the other man, his enemy?" I asked.

"He got safely to the little cottage and travelled by boat to his home the next day. He probably hated the young man more than ever."

"What became of the young man after that?" I wanted to know.

"He did not wish to be in the same neighbourhood as his enemy after that, so he left home and sailed away and never returned."

"Who was he?" I asked.

"We could say that his name was Abraham, but he likely knew that he would never be the father of many generations in his native land, so he went away from there. Indeed, there was no other choice but to go away—*burt, burt, BURT**. Now it is almost morning. It's time to finish our work and go home to sleep."

This was the story, if it was a story, that Abraham Burt told me. I have never forgotten it mainly because I felt, and I still feel, that he told it to me in Icelandic.

---

*Burt means 'go away' in Icelandic.

PATRICK O'MORE

L ate in the summer of 1879 a stranger arrived at the Icelandic settlement in Mooseland Hills, Nova Scotia. He asked for someone to accompany him to the mining town called Moose River Mines, which was about three or four miles from the settlement. He was rather odd-looking. He appeared to be about fifty years old with a big, black beard and very heavy eyebrows. His forehead was low, his nose thin and bent, and his eyes small, black and deep-set. There was something unusual about him that was hard to define. A restless expression in his eyes made him look like some sort of fugitive. He was never still and he rarely looked anyone in the eye when he was talking to him. He seemed to shift his gaze from one to another and he was rather unsteady, like someone who has been sick. Still, he walked fast. He wore a long cloak that had once been dark but was now faded and muddy. On his head he wore a broad-brimmed black hat, which contributed to his odd appearance. He carried a little case, and it must have been quite heavy because he kept switching it from one hand to the other.

Wherever he stopped in the settlement, he asked for milk to drink but he would not accept anything more. When he had finished drinking, he left one copper cent in the bowl but otherwise he did not thank people for the milk. No one in the settlement had seen him before and few paid much attention to him. I don't think that anyone even asked his name. I walked with him to Moose River Mines that day. I was thirteen years old and I knew enough English to understand the few words that he said to me on the way. Perhaps I should not say that I understood him completely because what he said was rather strange, but I knew the words themselves and I thought I understood what he was saying.

We started off from the settlement about noon and we followed a narrow and crooked trail, that led through the bush. It was quite hilly there, quite rough and not an easy path to take. There were large rocks here and there beside the way, and I noticed right away that this man paid particular attention to every stone we passed. He stopped beside some of the rocks, tried to move them, studied them from every aspect and put on the glasses that he carried in his vest pocket. The path to the mining town turned away from the main road just east of Copse Hill.

"What is this hill called?" asked the man after we took this path. Those were the first words he had spoken to me.

"Copse Hill," I said.

"This hill should have been called Corpse Knoll," he said, after we were about half a mile from the hill.

"Why?" I asked.

"Because here the wheel came apart beside the well twenty-five years ago," he said.

"The wheel came apart beside the well?" I asked, surprised.

"Yes, and here the silver cable was cut," he said, "and the young prospector gave up. He collapsed here beside the

path. I see his marks everywhere, everywhere, everywhere!"
He looked in all directions as he said this. I also looked all
around but I did not see any tracks except those of a barefoot Icelandic boy who had travelled that way in the
morning. I was wishing that I could get home again before
dusk.

"Here is Sesame!" said this strange man, as he pointed to
a big stone beside the path. "This is Sesame!" And he proceeded to study the stone from every angle. "Here is Sesame
and there is Sesame. They are everywhere. In each stone in
this area there is a hidden treasure, gold, gold, gold, bright,
beautiful gold! But we do not have the magic wand to open
these stones and we do not know the magic words." When
we had almost reached the mining town, he stopped all of a
sudden, took a small stone out of his pocket and showed it
to me. "Tell me now, my boy," he said, as he looked around
him, "tell me truly whether you have ever seen a stone like
this in this neighbourhood." I looked at the stone and I saw
nothing special about it, but I said, though, that I had never
seen a stone like it.

"I am surprised at that," said the man, "because young
people have sharp eyes. Now I do not need you to walk with
me any further because I can see the town over there." He
took five copper cents out of his pocket and counted them
out into my hand. "These are yours," he said. "That is a lot
of money for one who knows how to look after it. I would
like to give you one piece of advice. If you make a mistake in
something that you try to do, try again, not seven times but
seventy times seven."

I thanked him sincerely for the money and the advice and
said goodbye to him, glad that I could now turn back

towards home. When I had gone a few fathoms, he called out to me. "Listen, my boy, he said, "if ever you are travelling around Cole Harbour, do not forget to visit me."

"How shall I find your house?" I asked.

"Just ask for Father Patrick O'More," he said. "Everyone knows Father Patrick O'More." Then he continued on his way and I went mine.

Two years went by and I had long ago stopped thinking about the mysterious Father Patrick O'More. Then late in the summer I was sent on an errand to Halifax. I had planned to travel by ship from Tangier, which was the nearest port, but when I got there the ship had just left. I saw no other choice but to walk along the coast, about sixty miles. On the second day I came to a narrow inlet that reached far inland. Although I knew that it was not very far to the city and the sun was still high, I decided that I would not go much further that day. Near the inlet stood a fairly big store, and there were a few houses in the vicinity. I walked over to the store to inquire about a place to sleep. There were a few men gathered together there, and I judged that they were fishermen. "What is the name of this inlet?" I asked when I entered the store.

"It is called Cole Harbour," said a young man who stood at the counter smoking a short, clay pipe. It was clear from his accent that he was Irish. Then all of a sudden I remembered Father Patrick O'More and I thought that with him I would have a safe place to sleep.

"Doesn't Father Patrick O'More live nearby?" I asked.

"Yes, he lives here," said the Irishman, with a derisive smile. "You must be in need of some religious services since you are asking for Father Pat. Perhaps you have to baptize a child or something like that." I told him quite honestly that my business with Father Patrick O'More was of another kind altogether.

"So what business could you have with Father Pat, since you don't have to baptize a child or anything like that?" asked the Irishman, in the same mocking tone.

"I am going to ask to spend the night with him," I said. At that all the men burst into laughter.

"Have you ever heard the likes of that, fellows?" said the Irishman, as he took the pipe out of his mouth and looked towards the men who were gathered there. "He is just going to spend the night with Father Pat. Either the chap comes from the asylum or he is one of the lost sheep of the house of Israel. He is definitcly not Irish."

I was not pleased with this tomfoolery and I asked the men to direct me to the home of Father Patrick O'More. I also said that I had come a long way and that I was tired and did not care to listen to their jokes. The men stopped laughing and looked at each other.

"Do you know Father Patrick O'More, my boy?" asked the Irishman, trying to look serious at last.

"I saw him only once," I said.

"And do you know that at times he is stark, raving mad?" asked the Irishman.

"No," I said, and I thought to myself that he was joking. I said goodbye to the men and walked out. The Irishman came to the door and called to me. "If you must visit Father Patrick, my boy," he said, "his house is there up on the hillside just across from us. You would not be looking for a place to sleep there if you knew the man as well as we do."

I still thought that he was joking and I walked up the hill.

There stood a dilapidated log cabin with one little window. One pane was broken and was replaced by a wooden board. When I came a little closer I noticed that there were piles of stones all around the cabin, and obviously they had not been taken out of the ground around the cabin but had been brought in from elsewhere. I thought that this was not a very pleasant rectory and I began to think that the Irishman had fooled me and had not sent me to the Father's house but to some deserted cabin. I was almost ready to turn around without knocking but I did walk up to the cabin. When I was only a few feet away, the door was suddenly opened and Father Patrick stood on the threshold.

"Welcome, always welcome to my house!" he said, and he opened up his arms to greet me. "You are the boy who showed me the way from the Icelandic settlement to Moose River Mines. I often remember that time with gratitude, and I have often wished I could see you again, my love. And now you have come. My thoughts have drawn you to me. Faith moves mountains." Then I stepped into Father Patrick O'More's house.

Inside everything was very simple but still surprisingly clean. The furnishings consisted of one little table and two short benches, an old stove, a few pots and dishes, a bed, neatly made up, and a small bookcase with a few books in it. The books were mostly religious books and a few books dealing with geology. A copy of *A Thousand and One Nights* stood beside the Bible and looked as if it had been read more often than any of the other books. Obviously the Father lived there all by himself. He quickly cooked a supper, which consisted of oatmeal porridge with syrup, a few oatmeal cakes and a cup of tea.

While we ate this simple meal, he asked me who had directed me to his home. I told him that I had talked to a young man in the store down by the ocean and I tried to describe the man.

"That would have been my cousin Rory," he said, "and of course he told you that I was not in my right mind." I did not deny that the man had said something to that effect but I added quickly that I thought he was joking.

"They all think that I am mad," he said. "They all think that and they all call me Father Pat."

"Are you not a priest, then?"

"No," he said, and he shook his head sadly. " I am just called that because they scoff at me. Then he went on to tell his story.

When I was young I was a prospector and considered to be one of the wealthiest men hereabouts. I bought the Caribou Mines and spent a lot of money, and everything went well at first. Then all of a sudden I was out of funds and I lost almost everything I owned on that venture, for reasons that I do not have to explain. I was travelling through the area where the Icelandic settlement is now when I was told that I had lost everything. I have never recovered. Around the same time my mother died and my wife died soon after. I was left all alone and poor. I think I was crazy for a while. I was sick and bedridden for a long time. The doctors could not help me. Then suddenly I felt better, and at once I had a desire to preach to the people— preach love and forgiveness. I travelled among the people and preached, never expecting any remuneration. But people did not want to listen to my teaching. They smiled

*nicely, to be sure, but always let me know that they
thought I was crazy. Then I became disgusted with people
and felt that they were not as good as they pretended to be.
I found hypocrisy in many places. I found it in the marketplace and on the street corners, I found it in society and
in the church itself. I saw tears running down the cheeks
although the heart was happy, I saw men give to those in
difficult circumstances so that they could take advantage
of them later. I saw that friendships were often insincere
and that behind fair words there was often deceit.
Hypocrisy lurked everywhere, hypocrisy, hypocrisy,
hypocrisy, everywhere, more or less. That is mankind's
biggest sickness and it can never be completely cured. I
will not say that men are evil, but rather that as a rule they
are not as good as they pretend to be. Likely I have this
opinion of people because I am not of sound mind. Or perhaps something in one's mind has to snap before one can
see all this.*

*Anyway, I became disgusted with people and I began
to avoid them for the most part. I turned to stones instead
and offered them my preaching, not like the Venerable
Bede but rather as a scientist and prospector. I found that
the stones were straightforward. To be sure they were
hard, cold and without feeling, but always honest. I saw
that everywhere there were minerals, gold, silver, copper
or iron, and everywhere there was hidden treasure. Every
single stone was a little Sesame. Sesame, Sesame everywhere. I lacked nothing but the knowledge and secret of
how to open them and become another Midas. After I
had wandered through the woods for a few years I settled
here in this cabin because here I owned one hundred*

acres of uncleared land. These few acres were not thought to be worth anything and this land was the only possession that was not seized when I lost my money. There is an example of the kindness of the wealthy men who had power over me.

More than a hundred years ago a beautiful stone house was built on this very property, but now it has fallen into ruin and only a part of one gable end is still standing. According to an old story, there is buried treasure under the ruins. On one stone in the wall that still stands, some words were carved in a foreign language. Throughout two generations no one here could read the inscription. According to the old story, the message on the stone told where the treasure could be found. I copied the message onto a piece of paper as best I could and sent it off to several specialists in language, both in Halifax and Boston. Finally, I found out that the words were written in an old form of Polish and meant "A Polish exile built this house in 1739." Soon afterwards I met a Russian man who also knew Polish. I showed him the message and asked him to read the words backwards. Then the message could be taken in two different ways. 1739 became 9371 and the Polish word "house" when it was turned around spelt "gold." Then I found, as often before, that stones tell the truth.

"And what did all the words mean when they were read backwards?" I asked.

"I have never told anyone that, and I will never reveal that," he said.

"But the Russian man who translated the words for you,

he knows," I said.

"He knows the meaning of each word by itself, but he does not know the message in its entirety," said Patrick. "I had him first translate the word that was next to the last and then the word that was next to the first word, and I never let him see the order in which they were written on the stone and I never let him know anything about the date. Now the stone is no longer in the wall because I took it away and broke it into tiny pieces. Now that is my story."

As darkness fell that evening Patrick invited me to walk with him over to the ruins to examine them. When we got there he lit a lantern that he had been carrying. I saw that there were foundations of a large building but only a small part of one wall remained standing. All the rest had fallen and was overgrown with grass and weeds.

"There was the stone that I told you about," said Patrick, as he pointed to an opening in the middle of the wall, "and there are a few words carved into the stone which is on the right side of the opening. I know that they are in Icelandic because an Icelander wrote them when I went to Moose River Mines that year. My cousin Rory had him do that because the two of them were friends. Of course that was done to make fun of me. Now I want you to translate these words for me if you can read them."

I looked at the stone and saw that a few words were carved there. I tried again and again to make out the letters with no success. I could not read them because the letters were poorly drawn and did not look at all like Icelandic words.

"Can you read that?" asked Patrick.

"No," I said, "I am sure that is not written in Icelandic."

"That is strange because I am sure it is in Icelandic and it means 'Watch out! This man is crazy!' But I forgive the man who carved these words and I forgive my kinsman, Rory, not seven times, but seventy times seven." He sighed, blew out the lantern and invited me to come home with him. He made up a bed for me on the floor of the log cabin and he read a long prayer before he blew out the lamp.

I fell asleep at once and woke up just after sunrise. Then I noticed that Patrick wasn't in his bed and the bedclothes had not been disturbed. Soon after I woke up he came in and he was wearing mud-caked denim clothes. He looked as if he had been working in a mine overnight. He wished me a good morning; quickly prepared a meal similar to the one we had the evening before and had little to say.

When I had finished my breakfast I said goodbye to him and set off on my own journey. I never saw Patrick again.

Several years later I read a notice in a Halifax newspaper that reads, "Recently an old man from Cole Harbour passed away. His name was Patrick O'More, often known as Father Pat. In his younger days he was a well-to-do prospector and was owner of the infamous Caribou Mines near Upper Musquodoboit. He lost his fortune and became withdrawn after that. For a while he travelled around preaching the Gospel but later gave that up. Instead he began a search for hidden treasures, which he felt might be buried in the ground, especially where there were old ruins. For many years, he searched for a large fortune that he thought could be found near the ruins of an old castle in Cole Harbour. He dug fifteen or twenty holes, some quite deep, but never found the treasure.

"He was in many ways an intelligent man and well-informed about many subjects. His delusions were entirely related to the fact that he was convinced that treasures were hidden everywhere in the ground. He was like Don Quixote. Patrick O'More's will was found in his coffin. He willed to his cousin, Rory O'More, all that he owned, which was twenty-five dollars in copper and one hundred acres of untilled land in Cole Harbour."

HÁKON FARMANN

A few families from Iceland settled in Nova Scotia's
Mooseland Hills in the summer of 1875. They found
two clearings in the bush where prospectors had
been looking for gold. At both sites there were log cabins that
were only a few years old.

One of the camps was called Rider's Hill. An Englishman
named John Rider had spent two years searching for gold in
the highlands with little success. Many tall tales were told
about Rider and his escapades. On one occasion, he got lost
in the bush and he was near death when he was found.
Shortly after that, he returned to England with plans to go
prospecting in Australia.

The other clearing was a place that was referred to as
Sailor's Hill. The cabin there was quite large and had been
built recently. In 1873, a man who was known as Sinbad the
Sailor occupied it. Like John Rider, he had been digging for
gold in various places in the area. No one knew whether or
not he had actually found any. Many stories were told about
this man and usually he was depicted as a hero. Oddly
enough, no one knew his proper name. He was thought to
be either Danish or Dutch, and it was said that he had spent
years at sea. Hence, the nickname Sinbad the Sailor. He suddenly left Mooseland Hills, spent some time in Truro and

then left, it was thought, to return to Denmark or Holland.

The Icelandic settlers in Mooseland Hills knew of at least three countrymen who had spent some time in Nova Scotia before the settlement began. One of the three went back to Iceland and did not return from there. One had gone back to Iceland briefly and then emigrated from there to Manitoba. The third man had not been heard from and some guessed that he had gone to South America. During the last year that I lived in Nova Scotia, I briefly met an Icelandic man who was unknown to any of us in Mooseland Hills. I believe that he was the prospector called Sinbad the Sailor. Now I will tell you how I came to meet him.

One September day in 1881, when I was fifteen years old, I was on my way through the Musquodoboit Valley. I was sent to call on a Scottish farmer named Thomas Campbell. He lived on Maple Ridge, north of Lower Stewiacke, about thirty-five miles from the settlement. My errand with Mr. Campbell was to collect a few dollars that he owed my father. I set out walking very early in the morning, determined that I would reach Campbell's that evening, spend the night there and get home by nightfall the following day. I had never gone this way before, so I stopped often to ask directions when I got down into the valley. Because of this, the trip took longer than I expected. Several times that day, people had told me that just before Maple Ridge there was a big farm called Lindsay's Farm. I was advised to stop there and make sure I had clear directions because it was easy to lose one's way in those parts.

It was late afternoon when I reached Lindsay's Farm, a very prosperous-looking home. The house was big and impressive and stood quite far back from the road. At one time, two men from our group had been employed there and they had spoken highly of the family. I walked up to the house and knocked. An older woman, tall and stately, came to the door. This was Mrs. Lindsay herself, the owner of the farm. I greeted her and asked her if she would be so kind as to direct me to the home of Thomas Campbell. She received me politely and explained to me in detail how I should go. She pointed to a roadway, which lay up the hillside, and she told me to follow that path until I came to a bridge over the Moose River. I was not to go over the bridge but, rather, follow the road beside the river and then I would soon see Campbell's house. I thanked Mrs. Lindsay for her direction and said goodbye. "Tell me," she said, as I was leaving. "What is your name? Where have you come from?"

I told her my name and mentioned that I had come from the Mooseland Hills settlement.

"Have you walked all that way today?" she asked.

"Yes."

"And how old are you?"

"Going on sixteen," I told her.

"I don't want you to go any further this evening," said Mrs. Lindsay. "It is four miles to Campbell's and soon it will be dark. You are tired and hungry. Stay here tonight."

I thanked her for her kind offer but I told her that I must get to Campbell's that evening. I said I wasn't tired or hungry and it was nothing to run another four miles. Then she offered me a cup of milk, which I accepted gratefully. She asked again whether I wouldn't stay the night or wait until the men returned from the hayfields with the horses. Then they could take me in a cart to Campbell's. I thanked her for her kind offers but I repeated that I was not tired and I set out with determination. "Don't forget. Do not cross the bridge. Follow the river on the east side," she called out. I said I would remember. When I looked back a few minutes later, I saw that Mrs. Lindsay was still standing outside watching me.

When I reached the top of the hill, the sun was about to set but the moon was coming up. Now the path led through a thick forest and I began to regret that I had not accepted Mrs. Lindsay's kind invitation. However, I tried to keep up my courage and I hurried more than ever. I had not gone far when I heard horses' hooves further west and the sounds were coming closer. As I came around a bend in the road, I saw a man on a white horse approaching. I moved out to the side of the road to let him pass but, instead of continuing, he stopped, got down from the horse and proceeded to adjust his saddle. I thought he looked quite young and strong but I could not see him clearly at all and, besides, he was wearing a broad-brimmed hat. I greeted him and he answered briefly, as he continued to fix his saddle.

"What became of the man who was with you?" he asked.

"There was no one with me," I said.

"You can't tell me that," he said, raising his voice slightly. "I saw two men come around the bend in the road and one walked with a cane but now he has disappeared. He must have jumped into the bush just as I got off the horse."

I said that I was alone and I had not seen anyone since I left Lindsay's Farm until I met him. He looked at me and said that he could not believe that.

"Where have you come from?" he asked. I answered his question.

"Aren't you worried about travelling alone at night in the bush?"

"No," I said. "What is there to be afraid of?"

"Of the dark and of the forest itself. Lots of creatures live in the forest."

"Are there bears in these woods?" I asked.

"They are seldom seen around here."

"What is there to be afraid of?" I asked again.

"Some might think that robbers could be travelling around at night."

"I don't have to fear any robbers," I said, "because I don't have any money."

"But any robbers you might meet would think that you had money, since you are a traveller, and they might search your pockets to check it out."

"And they would find nothing in my pockets but an old jack-knife," I said.

"Then they would take the knife for sure."

"Not if I can help it," I said, trying to be brave in the face of this conversation.

"Oh," he said. "You'd have me believe that you're no sissy. Where are you going?"

"To Mr. Campbell's. Is it much further now?"

"Only half a mile. It is the first house that you come to on the west side of the river."

"But I was told that his home was on the east side of the river and that I should not cross the bridge," I said.

"Who told you that?"

"Mrs. Lindsay."

"You have misunderstood her, or Mrs. Lindsay was not clear about it, because you have to keep on going west over the bridge to come to Campbell's. The house is only about a hundred yards from the river, right beside the road." As he said this, he climbed on his horse and took off at a pace down the path toward the east.

I continued west along the ridge and hurried. Soon I got to the bridge over the Moose River, which flowed through a deep gorge. The river is huge in the spring but, at this time, the water was low. At the gorge, I paused to consider what I should do. Should I take the road over the bridge or take the road that followed the river on the east side? Finally, I decided that I would continue over the bridge because I thought I could hear people talking not far away on the west side of the river. Soon after I had crossed the bridge I noticed a light nearby. I was close to a big barn and then I saw the farmhouse near the road. I felt sure that this was the home of Thomas Campbell. Near the barn, I saw a woman with a milk pail in her hand and a little girl who was carrying a lantern. I greeted them and asked the woman whether Thomas Campbell lived there.

"No," she said. "Thomas Campbell lives on the east side of the river, about half a mile from the bridge. This is the home of Duncan Campbell. What is your name and where have you come from?"

I answered her questions and told her that Mrs. Lindsay had given me directions and told me not to cross the bridge, but that I had met a young man on a white horse on the ridge and he had said that Campbell lived on the west side of the river. I had followed his advice. I added that I was glad to know that I had not gone far out of my way and now I would not have any difficulty in finding my way to Thomas Campbell's farm.

As I was turning to leave, the woman said, "You would be better off to stay here for the night. You have travelled far enough today and you are tired. First thing tomorrow morning you can see Thomas Campbell. The man on the white horse whom you met this evening is my son, Duncan. He must have intended that you spend the night here because he knows that Thomas and all his folk are planning to attend a performance at the schoolhouse down in the valley. They will not be home much before dawn so I want you to stay here tonight."

I accepted her kind offer and, in truth, I was thankful for a chance to rest by this time for I was tired and hungry. I walked into the house with the woman and the little girl.

Later on I learned that this woman was the widow of Malcolm Campbell. He had been a ship's captain for a long time and was well known throughout Nova Scotia. He had made his home in Dartmouth but he had died shortly before the Icelandic group arrived in this province. At this time, Mrs. Campbell lived on the farm with her two sons, Duncan and Robert.

Mrs. Campbell offered me a seat at the table and soon she brought me food and drink. She told me that she and the little girl would also be going to the program at the school and her two sons would be there as well. She said she would make up a bed for me on the couch before she left and I could take my rest whenever I was ready. "When you wake up in the morning, we will all be home again," she said. "But, before you go to sleep, you could talk to Mr. Farmann if you like. He is not going to go to the school tonight. He is Icelandic like you."

"Do I understand that an Icelandic man is living here?" I was excited.

"Yes, and I am sure he would enjoy talking to you. He has not been with Icelandic people for a long time. I have let him know that you will be spending the night here." As soon as I finished eating, Mrs. Campbell told me to come with her to meet Mr. Farmann. I was happy to do that. Mrs. Campbell gave a little knock on his door and said, "Mr. Farmann, I have brought the boy that I told you about earlier."

The door opened at once and I saw an older man, rather short and quite lean and a little stooped. He had a no-nonsense look about him, but still, he seemed pleasant. His hair was silver as was his beard, which was cut short. "I will look after the boy, Mrs. Campbell," he said kindly. Then he greeted me in Icelandic, shook my hand, and invited me into his room. Mrs. Campbell said goodnight and left the two of us together.

Mr. Farmann's room was quite spacious. He had a good bed, a large bookcase, a fine writing desk, an Icelandic *koffort* and two chairs. On his desk, there was a nice-looking lamp and some newspapers that he had been reading. "Mr. Farmann, I hardly expected that I would be meeting another Icelander here tonight," I said.

"You can call me Hákon," he said. "That is my Christian name."

"And whose son are you?" I asked.

"I have been called Farmann since I came to this country because I spent long years at sea like the old Vikings," he said.

"But what was your father's name?"

"I am sure you've never heard of him," he said, as he folded up some of the papers on his desk.

"I didn't think there were any Icelanders in this part of the province."

"Circumstances decided that we would meet here tonight," he said, good-naturedly. "This morning you left Mooseland Hills with a plan to reach Thomas Campbell's home and spend the night there. And, this morning, I was busy making hay in the valley to the west of us. I did not expect to come back here for three days. Things happened so that I had to come back at noon today and stay here until tomorrow morning. Also, circumstances arranged that you met a man on the ridge and he sent you over here. Coincidences are often amazing and we do not understand the laws that govern them."

"Have you been in Musquodoboit for a long time?" I asked.

"I had already spent about three years in Nova Scotia before the group settled in Mooseland Hills. Something happened that caused me to stay in this province rather than go to Utah or Wisconsin. Ever since I was a small boy, things have kept happening to change my decisions and my plans for the future. Therefore, I have never been able to reach the goals that I have set for myself."

"What happened to make you decide to stay in Nova Scotia?" I asked, a little hesitantly.

"It was such a small thing that it is not worth talking about it but, on account of that, I began to dig for gold in the hills just where the Icelandic settlers are now living. I built a cabin for myself near the Tangier River, about three miles from the hill where the Englishman John Rider had his camp. You must have heard about Rider's Hill."

"Yes. I have heard many stories about John Rider. I have

also heard stories about a mysterious prospector who was called Sinbad the Sailor."

"Oh, is that so?" said Hákon. "Well, John Rider certainly was a strange man. He searched for gold in Mooseland Hills but never found any. He seemed to be knocked back and forth by circumstances. They finally drove him, more dead than alive, away from the hills. He had left long before I came there."

"Did you find gold?" I asked.

"I was there for only one year. The hand of fate again prevented me from staying on there any longer."

"Were you not allowed to search for gold?" I asked. I wanted to know more about this man's life and I hoped he would tell me briefly how things had turned out for him.

"Why would I not be allowed to continue my search?" he asked, and his eyes flashed. "I got hurt. It was midwinter, I was helpless and I was a good twenty miles from any homes."

"How did you get hurt? Did you break a leg or cut your foot with an axe?"

"It doesn't matter how it happened," said Hákon, rather sharply. "I was hurt and could not look after myself. Then came unexpected help. A young hunter who had been out in the hills came to my cabin just by coincidence. He offered to move me out of the bush to get help. He had brought a light sleigh with him and he used that to haul me away after he bundled me up with blankets. He pulled the sleigh over a narrow, crooked path through the bush, all the way over the ridge and down to the Musquodoboit Valley. That was quite an effort because we travelled through heavy snow all the way. He started off in the evening because it was a moonlit night. Just at daybreak, we reached the doctor's home. That saved my life. The young man who proved to be such a good friend was the same young man whom you met on the ridge this evening and who sent you here. He was my Good Samaritan. Comparing him to other young men is like comparing gold to copper."

"Were you sick for a long time?" I inquired.

"I was in bed for seven weeks. During that time, my new friend visited me every day. He lived more than four miles from the inn where I stayed to recuperate."

"So you came here after you recovered?"

"After the accident, I spent almost two years in Truro. I managed to save a bit of money and I had decided definitely that I would go back to Iceland in the fall of 1875. Then, something happened that made me change my mind. I decided against going to Iceland and my good friend Duncan asked me to come and stay here for as long as I wanted. I accepted his offer and here I will spend the rest of my days because I am so content."

"But why did you give up your plan to return to Iceland?" As if he had not heard my question, Hákon jumped up, opened the door and looked out into the hall.

"Yes, they are leaving now, Mrs. Campbell and little Maria," he said. "They are going to the school." He closed the door again and sat down at his desk. I wanted to repeat my question but he started asking about conditions in the settlement. He wanted to know who had left during the summer to go to the Red River Valley and he wanted to know when the others planned to leave. He agreed that it would be a good idea to leave the Mooseland Hills, but he said he was sure that the settlers had, nevertheless, learned a lot from their experience. "Circumstances brought them to the hills and some force beyond our control is now moving them away again. Whoever governs these events is wise and there are reasons for everything. That unseen hand is mighty and infallible."

"I do not understand that. But I would like to know why you decided not to return to Iceland."

"Listen. I think I hear a knock at the front door," he said, and he walked out into the front hall. He returned quickly. "Oh, it was just the wind," he said. Then he said, "Once again I will tell you that everything that lives and moves on earth is affected by unforeseen events and coincidences. In my younger days I knew a man who was quite promising, but strange events followed him in such a way that most of his plans and his decisions were altered. He grew up with indulgent parents in his father's old family home. He always planned to seek higher education, to qualify for a good position, to become well off and to maintain his father's property as well as possible. But circumstances changed things in such a way that he barely learned to read and write, he was always poor, he never married, he went to sea on a merchant ship and visited many harbours. He was always a stranger and a foreigner. In his later years, he settled down with good people of a nationality other than his own in a secluded valley in a prosperous land. After a long life, the only thing he had gained was the knowledge that some good and wise people cared about him. This is the best that one can gain from life and it is worth a lot. Now do you understand?"

"Yes," I said, but I felt that I was far from understanding this unusual man.

Presently Hákon said that I should get ready for bed for I

must be tired and in need of sleep. He walked with me into
the dining room, lit a lamp for me and checked to see that
my bed was ready on the couch. "When you get up in the
morning, I will be on my way," said Hákon, "because tomorrow I will be busy with the hay down in the valley. We will
not likely meet again since you will soon be leaving for
Winnipeg and I will remain here. You wanted to know what
my position was here—whether I was a hired man or working for myself. All I can tell you is that this is my home and I
am as free as the air I breathe. Everyone is good to me, but
Duncan is best of all. Before I say goodbye and bid you goodnight, I would like to let you hear a refrain from an old
ballad." He repeated two lines from an old ballad over three
or four times:

> *Utan eftir firðinum, sigla fagrar fleyr,*
> *Sá er enginn glaður eftir annan þreyr.*

Then he took my hand, said goodnight, walked to the
door, looked back for a moment, said goodnight once more
and went into his room. I never saw him again. I got up early
the next morning but, sure enough, he had already left for the
hayfields.

While I had breakfast, Mrs. Campbell talked about various things but she avoided any mention of Hákon. I tried
again and again to ask about him but her answers were
always such that I really learned nothing more. Still, I felt
that she thought well of Hákon and she indicated that she
and her sons appreciated him.

After breakfast, I set off again. Mrs. Campbell walked with
me to the bridge over the Moose River and showed me the

road that followed the gorge. I said goodbye to this kind
Scottish woman and thanked her for her hospitality.

After about fifteen minutes, I arrived at Thomas
Campbell's home. He also had a prosperous-looking farm
there on the ridge. I explained the reason for my coming. He
invited me to spend the day with his family and leave the
next morning. I told him that I had to get home that evening
because my father was leaving for Winnipeg. Then Mr.
Campbell gave me the money that he owed my father and he
took me, with horse and cart, about ten miles north along
the Musquodoboit Valley. On the way, he was quite talkative
and often quite witty and full of jokes, even though he was
getting up in years. He told me stories about Robbie Burns
and recited many of his poems. Finally, the conversation
turned to Hákon and the family that he lived with. I felt right
away that Thomas Campbell had a lot of respect for his
neighbours. Indeed, they were close relatives. And he had
only praise for the Icelander.

"Mr. Farmann is somewhat unusual in his ways," said Mr.
Campbell. "But he is, nevertheless, a fine man and well
informed about many things. He has told us that Nova
Scotia is the land that his forefathers discovered centuries
ago and named Vinland, not Markland as some people
believe, but Vinland. These could be just his own beliefs, but
it could also be the truth. We cannot debate that point, lad. I
have known Mr. Farmann for more than six years and all I
have known of him has been good. He was not content in
this country at first and was determined to go home in the
fall of 1875. But then, all of a sudden, he changed his mind."

"Do you know why he decided not to go to Iceland?" I
asked.

"Yes, I know that for certain," said Mr. Campbell. "He put forth all his money, about five hundred dollars, to help Duncan Campbell and his brother out of debt. Mr. Farmann considered that Duncan had saved his life when he was injured out in the bush about twenty miles away from any help. It happened that a gun that Farmann was handling accidentally discharged and he was badly wounded in the shoulder. After he recovered somewhat, he went to Truro and found suitable work there. In two years' time, he had set aside five hundred dollars. He decided that he would return to Iceland. He came here in September of 1875 to say good-bye to Duncan and discovered that the brothers were in debt and would have to sell almost everything that they owned, including two white horses that were special to them. When Mr. Farmann saw how things were, he changed his mind about going to Iceland and, instead, he asked his friend Duncan to take his money to cover the debt. Duncan accepted the offer but only on the condition that Mr. Farmann would make his home with them. Mr. Farmann moved in with them in the fall and he has been like one of the family since. The Campbells are now well off, in large measure because of the help of this good Icelander. He does seem a little strange at times and he believes strongly in fate."

I said goodbye to Thomas Campbell shortly before noon and still had twenty-five miles to walk, but I did get home that evening. All the way home, I was thinking about the strange verse that Hákon repeated over and over as he said goodbye to me. I could not grasp the meaning then but now I think I know what he meant. Perhaps Hákon was conveying the idea that coming "home" holds little joy when one's loved ones are no longer there.

BERGLJÓT

The week before Whitsunday in the spring of 1882 I said my last goodbye to Mooseland Hills, Nova Scotia, and set out for Winnipeg. A few days earlier my mother's belongings had been sent to Stewiacke, which was the nearest railway station. My mother and my sister planned to get there on the Monday after Whitsunday. They would wait there while I went to Halifax to buy the tickets.

On my way to the city I had to stop at Dartmouth. There I had to find a young man named Daniel Campbell. His father had been our neighbour for some years and he bought most of the household articles and tools that we wanted to sell before we left. He owed us a few dollars and I was to collect those from Daniel, who was working for a clergyman near Dartmouth.

As it happened, Daniel was not at home when I arrived at the parsonage. That very day he had been sent on an errand to Truro and he was not expected back until Saturday night at the earliest. Naturally, I was sorry to learn that he was away and I thought I would go to Halifax and then come back to Dartmouth on Saturday. The pastor and his wife would not hear of that and insisted instead that I should stay with them until Daniel returned. In the end, I agreed to stay there until Monday.

In spite of this hospitality, I knew I would have time on my hands. First of all, there were no young people there. Secondly, there were two older ladies visiting them, and the pastor and his wife had to devote time to their guests. I spent a quiet evening, but the pastor's wife brought the suggestion that I should explore the town the next day but come back to the parsonage in time for meals. I saw that this was a good idea.

Right after breakfast the next day, I set out on my sight-seeing tour. First of all, I walked down by the sea and then followed the river, which runs through the northern part of the town. I knew that nearby was a famous old factory where firearms of various kinds were manufactured. I had thought I would like to go there, but on my way I stopped beside a little house that stood near the riverbank. The house was probably about twelve feet by sixteen feet and was built in the form of a shanty. In fact, it looked like it might originally have been a porch or a lean-to on a bigger building. It had recently been painted white. There were two windows, one on each end, and a door that faced the street. Around the house was a low rail fence. Two huge elm trees stood on guard, one at each end of the house. The branches grew over the roof of the house as if to protect it from rain, wind or summer heat. I stopped there, not because the house was so impressive or the rail fence was so low or the elm trees so tall. It was because I saw two children, a girl and a boy, come out of the house. To my surprise, they were speaking Icelandic. The children looked to be about the same age, probably about five or six years old. They had golden hair and red cheeks like healthy youngsters who grow up with good air and plenty of sunshine. They walked out to the street and immediately turned and ran to one of the windows, which was half open.

"She's coming! She's coming!" they said clearly in Icelandic.

Just then a frail-looking old woman walked up to the house and spoke to the children in English. She went directly into the house and the children followed her. A few moments later a young woman, rather slight, stepped out of the door. She was wearing a light-coloured cotton dress and a straw hat and she carried a small package. She did not look to right or left but hurried out of the yard and started off down the street half running. It was obvious that she was in a hurry. I was very surprised because I had never heard of any Icelandic people living in Dartmouth. Also, I thought that all the Icelandic families in the area had left except for one older couple who had made their home in Halifax. I felt like going up to the house to make some inquiries but I hesitated. However, I decided against going to the firearms plant and returned instead to the parsonage. I asked the pastor whether he knew of any Icelandic people in the neighbourhood. He said that he had not heard of any. In fact, he said that I was the only Icelandic person that he had ever laid eyes on.

After lunch I went for a walk again and I passed the little house several times, but I did not catch sight of the children.

Early the next morning I walked along the river again and was almost up to the rail fence when I saw the same young woman. She was coming down the street dressed as she was the day before and carrying a small parcel under one arm. She was obviously in a hurry. I pulled myself together, crossed her path, lifted my hat and said good morning to her. She answered me politely and paused.

"Is there an Icelandic family living in this house?" I asked in English.

"Why do you ask?" She frowned slightly.

"You are probably Icelandic," I said in my own language. She was a little taken aback, but her frown disappeared and she looked very interested.

"Yes, I am Icelandic," she answered in our familiar tongue, "but I am surprised to hear Icelandic spoken out on the street in Dartmouth." I explained my business in the town and I also told her how I had happened to discover that Icelandic people lived in this house. She said that she was happy to meet one of her countrymen but she could not stop to chat just then because she was on her way to work. Instead, she invited me to look in the next day, Sunday, at noon when she would be home. I thanked her for the invitation and promised to come. Then she said goodbye and hurried eastward into the town. When I passed the house, I saw that the children were in the garden and the old woman was with them. She was talking to them in English.

I returned to the parsonage just before noon and stayed there for the rest of the day. The day passed with no sign of Daniel. I started to worry that I would miss him altogether because I had made all my plans for our departure for Manitoba. That is exactly what happened. I was disappointed at the time because I did not see Daniel, but I decided that I would stay at the parsonage until Monday because I was looking forward to the visit on Sunday afternoon. However, I must add that the money that was owed was sent by mail and reached us later that summer in Winnipeg.

On Whitsunday, I went to church in the morning and then, about two o'clock, I set out on my own. When I arrived at the little house, the young woman was waiting at the doorway to welcome me. There were only two small rooms in the house; one for sleeping and one for kitchen, dining and living space. The furnishings were simple but the house was neat and clean. The two young children were there but there was no sign of the old woman.

I wondered if there was a man about the house but I saw nothing that would indicate that was the case. I could not help feeling very curious about the circumstances of this woman and the children but I tried to restrain myself from asking too many questions.

The woman introduced herself as Bergljót but I don't recall whose daughter she was. I don't think I asked her where she grew up in Iceland. Now I got a clearer impression of her because she had been wearing a wide-brimmed hat when I saw her on her way to work.

She was rather small and her face was pale. She had thick black hair and dark eyes. There was something about her expression and her bearing that commanded respect. I was only fifteen years old at the time but somehow I felt quite sure that here was a woman who would be passionate in love or in anger.

While she was making the coffee, she asked me several questions about my forthcoming trip to the West. I had the feeling that she would have liked to have gone to the Red River Valley herself. The children listened to our conversation, quiet and polite, and obviously they thought it unusual

to have a guest who could speak their native language. After
we sat down to drink our coffee, I tried to ask the odd question that would help me to understand her situation.

"Is your husband away?" I ventured.

"My husband?" She looked me straight in the eye. "I
don't have a husband."

"Did he die?" I asked, warily.

"I have never had a husband. I have never been married,"
she said, rather irritably. "Why do you ask?"

I flushed a bit and didn't answer but, in spite of myself, I
looked toward the children.

"Oh, the children," she said then, and smiled.

"Yes. Aren't they your children?" I asked, feeling now that
I was asking too many questions.

"Yes, they are my children. I am their Mama but not their
mother," she said then.

"Did their mother die?"

"Yes, and their father also," she answered in a low voice,
which suggested that she did not want to talk much about
that. But my curiosity was not satisfied.

"So you were related to one of the parents?" I asked.

"No, I was working for them in Iceland."

"Did they die in Iceland?"

"They both died in Halifax. He died just after he arrived
there and she died a couple of years ago."

"Did you come with them from Iceland?" I asked,
because I still wanted answers.

"Yes, we all planned to go to Manitoba but we did not
have the funds to go any further."

"How many years have you been in this country?"

"It will be five years this fall."

"Don't you still want to go to Winnipeg?"

"It's no use wanting something that you know you cannot afford," she said. "I had earned enough money to go and was planning to leave but then she died."

"The mother?"

"Yes."

"You must have looked after her and the children while she was ill and then looked after her funeral."

"I spent all the money that fall."

"So you have adopted the children?"

"She asked me to make sure that they would not be placed in an institution. Besides, I was fond of the children."

"Have you given up the idea of going west altogether?"

"I don't have the money for that anymore."

"Didn't you have any relatives here who could help to pay your way?"

"Yes, I had a relative," she said.

"Who was he? What was his name?"

"It does not matter what his name was."

"Was he a young man?"

"About my age."

"Couldn't he help you?" I asked.

"I wrote to him and told him about my financial circumstances and about the children I had adopted."

"So, what did he say?"

"He said he would gladly help me to get to Winnipeg and he advised me to get the children into an orphanage in Halifax. I wrote him back and told him that I would not abandon the children."

"What did he do then?"

"I got no reply."

"And he has not written since?"

"No."

We said nothing more for a while. I would have liked to ask more questions but I felt that I had gone far enough. Afterwards we talked of this and that. She said she was going to teach the children to read Icelandic before she sent them to public school. She said that her main goal was to help them to get a good education. She worked in a laundry six days a week but the wages were low. She was not able to save much but still she had managed a down payment on the little house. She said she would have it all paid for in two years if she were able to work full time. She had arranged for an older Scottish woman to stay with the children during her working days. She paid this woman one dollar each week for her help.

I asked Bergljót whether I might tell the pastor and his wife about her because they might be able to lend a helping hand. She refused, saying that she did not want any help with the children as long as she was healthy. She certainly did not want me to inquire about her relative when I got to the Red River Valley. She said she had no message for him or anyone else out there.

When I was leaving, she and the children walked out into the garden with me. I pointed to the elm trees and told her that I thought they were beautiful.

"When it storms, the trees are likely to fall and cause a lot of damage," she said.

"They will fall into the river rather than on the house," I suggested.

"But they will lift up the house at the same time because the largest roots go right under it."

I said goodbye to Bergljót and the children and headed back to the parsonage. I did not see or hear of them again, but I often thought about her and wondered how they had managed.

H A F L I ð I

When it comes to Icelanders in Nova Scotia, I can't forget to mention a man named Hafliði who was known as Harris after he immigrated. Actually, I do not have much to tell since he never came to the settlement at Mooseland Hills and the people there did not know him. He had already spent some time in this country when our group arrived in Nova Scotia in 1875. He may have been with the group who moved from Ontario to Nova Scotia in the fall of 1874. He first settled near Truro, then he went to Halifax and Dartmouth.

Sometimes when people from the settlement travelled through the beautiful Musquodoboit Valley west of Mooseland Hills, they were asked if they knew an Icelander who was called Harris. This happened most often at the store in Upper Musquodoboit. Our people bought supplies at that store once in a while and, at one time, we even received our mail there. A group of us boys were at the store one day in 1881 and we were asked whether we had met a man on the road just east of the town. We said no, we had not seen anyone since we came down into the valley. "There was an Icelandic man here just after twelve o'clock today," said the storekeeper, as he was filling our orders, "and he just left to go north out of the valley. He said his name was Harris and he was on his way from Dartmouth to Truro. Do you know him?" We said that we had never heard of him. "He is rather a small man," said the storekeeper, "but he is very quick and undoubtedly he is used to travelling on foot and making good time. He left Dartmouth this morning and he expects to be in Truro by midnight. The distance from Dartmouth to Truro is about sixty miles. He has travelled through here every fall for the past four or five years. He always comes from Dartmouth and he is always on his way to Truro. He always takes the road on the east side of the mountain when he is going north, but he takes the road on the west side of the mountain when he is coming southward." We doubted that this man was Icelandic. At any rate, his name, Harris, was certainly not Icelandic.

"He is Icelandic from head to toe," said the storekeeper. "He has the look of an Icelander and he speaks with the same accent. He is undoubtedly a kind man and loyal. I have twice asked him what business he has in Truro every fall. Both times his answer was the same: 'There is a little boy in Truro.' The last time I saw him, he said, 'Please do not forget me.'"

Other stories that the storekeeper told about Harris left us wondering about this man. Before long, I had the opportunity to get to know him a little bit.

Now I must explain that at the beginning of 1882, when I was fifteen years old, I started work at a lumber camp. I arrived there late one afternoon. I had walked more than fifteen miles and the road had been almost impassable in places because of the heavy snowfall. I remember how thankful I was to get into the warmth of the camp. The long log house was also quite wide, but the roof seemed rather low. In the middle of the dirt floor was a fireplace, and there was a large opening in the ridge of the roof to let out the smoke. There were long benches on either side of the fire and up against the walls were the bunks where the men slept. At one end of the building was a cookstove and there were two tables where twenty men could take their meals. The one big room served as kitchen, pantry, dining room, living room and sleeping quarters. This was Cameron's Lumber Camp.

The lumberjacks received me well and were always good to me. There were seventeen men there. Our employer, Mr. Cameron, was there when I arrived but he went home the day after, leaving his nephew, Grant, to take his place as overseer. Cameron's home was about twenty miles away from the camp.

In my mind I can still see these good men as they sat on the benches on either side of the fire when I walked in that first afternoon. They were all young men, energetic and good-humoured. I became acquainted quickly and I liked them all. On the first evening I learned that one of the men was an Icelander by the name of Hafliði but known by his fellow workers as Harris the teamster. He was one of the three men who hauled the logs down to the riverbank. He had two horses; one was a roan and the other was dapple grey. These two horses were thought to be Cameron's best horses, especially the grey. Hafliði was fond of the horses and he took good care of them.

Hafliði was probably in his late thirties, rather small and lean but fleet of foot. He was fair-haired and blue-eyed. I took to him immediately because he was kindly and well-meaning in demeanour. We often exchanged words in Icelandic or chatted a bit when time and circumstance allowed. He was quite talkative and well-informed and always pleasant. Sometimes he would even tease a little, but always in good fun. His English was not always grammatically correct but, still, he spoke without hesitation and the lumberjacks seemed to understand him very well. If any one of them said something to him in fun or as a joke, he always had a quick answer that got a laugh. All the men in the camp seemed to respect Hafliði, even more so after the event that I am going to relate to you now.

As I mentioned before, our employer, Mr. Cameron, went home the day after I came to the camp. His nephew, Grant, was left in charge of the workers. Grant was about twenty-five years old, solid looking, cheerful and pleasant in manner, and all the men were on good terms with him.

Early one Sunday morning in mid-January, Grant said that he would like to have someone go to Reid's farm, which was on the east side of the Musquodoboit Valley about eight miles from the camp. "My uncle promised to send me a package with various small items and he said he would get the package to Reid's last weekend. I was to pick it up there, but today I have to walk up the riverbank to check the evergreens up at the point. Bob and Frank will go with me. Who will go out west into the valley to Reid's place to get my package?"

"I will get the parcel if I can have a horse to ride," said a strong-looking man named Donald.

"Yes, of course you can have a horse," said Grant. "I certainly wouldn't expect you to go on foot."

"I wouldn't want any of the horses except the dapple grey," said Donald, "because he is a trusty horse and good for riding."

"Of course you can have whichever horse you trust the best," said Grant. At this point, Hafliði spoke up.

"May I have a word?" he asked.

"Of course," said Grant, smiling good-humouredly. "And what do you have to say?"

"I do not want to lend the dapple grey today," he said. "And not the roan either." All the lumbermen stared when they heard this comment.

"How is this, my good Harris?" asked Grant. "Do you own the horses?"

"No, I do not own them."

"Who owns them?" asked Grant.

"Mr. Cameron, your uncle, owns them," said Hafliði calmly, "and he has given me the duty of working the horses and looking after them this winter."

"But my uncle has put me in his place," said Grant quietly, "to supervise you, his workers, and I guess that means that I also decide what work the horses do."

"But just the same, it is clear to you, I hope, that you must not abuse the rights of the horses any more than you would abuse the rights of the men," said Hafliði, smiling.

"I'm afraid I don't understand you," said Grant, looking directly into Hafliði's face. "Or do you mean that I do not have the right to have my uncle's horses work for me?"

"I believe," said Hafliði, "that you could have lent out the dapple grey or indeed any or all of the horses yesterday, which was a working day, and you could lend them all out tomorrow, which is a working day, but absolutely not today because today is a day of rest. Do you understand me?"

"I am not sure that I understand you fully," said Grant. "It seems to me that it would not hurt any horse in good shape to carry a man a few miles, whether it is a working day or the Sabbath."

"Allow me to explain this better," said Haflidi, and he spoke slowly and calmly. "The horses that are in my care haul heavy loads from morning to night for six days each week. They get no pay like you and I except for feed and shelter. They are entitled to one day each week to rest. They have a right to be left in peace for that day, or what do you think? Now do you understand me?"

"Yes, I think I understand what you are saying," said Grant, after a moment's reflection, "and no doubt you have a point. Nevertheless, I need today to get this package that is waiting for me at Reid's. It is quite a long way to Reid's farm, likely the road is almost impassable and the package probably weighs twenty pounds. I cannot imagine that either you, Harris, or anyone else in this camp would care to set out on foot."

"I will go for you," said Haflidi. "I will go at once."

"Well and good," said Grant. "That is decided then. But think carefully whether it would not be as well to have the dapple grey along for the trip." Haflidi did not answer but he moved over to a man named Miller who was sitting at the table. He asked Miller to look after the horses while he was away. A few moments later, Haflidi had set out on foot for Reid's farm. The road he had to follow led through thick bush. Grant left about the same time with three men to check the forest further up the Moose River. The tract that they were to examine was about two miles from the camp. They all set out just about the time that the sun was rising. Grant and the men who were with him came back about noon. At that time, there were only a few degrees of frost and the winds were calm but snow was falling thick and fast. While the men were having their noon meal, Grant said that Harris would find it heavy going through the bush and he probably would not travel more than two miles each hour so he would take four hours each way. "I don't expect Harris will be here before six o'clock in the evening, at the earliest," said Grant, "although I'm sure that he can walk with the best of them." Some of the men said that he would hardly be back before eight or nine o'clock.

All day long the snow continued, and towards evening the winds started up. By seven o'clock, when we had our supper, Hafliði had not arrived. Eight o'clock came, but no Hafliði. Grant became restless and anxious, I thought, and he had little to say. He often went out in the evening and looked in the direction of the road to Reid's. There was little to see but darkness and snow. The whole evening passed and still Hafliði did not come. We all went to sleep late that night. At dawn the next day, the snow finally let up. When we got up, the weather was cool and clear but Hafliði was not back. Grant talked about sending two men to search for him after breakfast.

Just as we were about to leave the table, the camp door suddenly opened and in walked Hafliði. He held a parcel under one arm. He looked rather tired but he stepped in quickly and wished us all good morning quite cheerfully. He handed the parcel to Grant and also a letter, which he pulled out of his pocket. We all greeted Hafliði with great relief. "What is this?" said Grant, when he had read the letter. "Is it possible that you went all the way to my uncle's home?"

"Yes," said Hafliði. "Yesterday when I came to Reid's there was no parcel there for you and I did not feel like returning without it, so I decided I would have to go and see your uncle. I rested there for a good hour and enjoyed an excellent dinner. Meanwhile your uncle had written the letter, which he asked me to deliver to you when he gave me the package. Then I set out for the return trip and here I am safe and sound. And has everything gone well here? As they say, all's well that ends well."

"Things have turned out better than we feared for a while," said Grant. "Now you rest for today. You need it after walking forty-three miles in heavy snow in twenty-two hours. We'll say no more."

Hafliði lay down after breakfast and rested until noon. He worked all afternoon until evening and he showed no signs of exhaustion. During the evening, I managed to exchange a few words with him in Icelandic. I asked what possessed him, what made him think of travelling that distance on foot. "If I had not done this," he said, "my grey horse would not have had a rest on Sunday for the rest of the winter." That was his reply.

During the next few days, the workmen tried to guess what Cameron's letter to Grant had been about. Most thought it had been all about the treatment of his horses.

As I mentioned earlier, I came to work in Cameron's camp at the beginning of January of 1882 and I was there for about three months. The longer I was there, the better I liked the men who worked there. They were all so good to me and they were all well-meaning. But I especially liked Hafliði, likely because he happened to be Icelandic. He must have felt at times that I was too curious about things and asked too many questions. Still, he answered my queries patiently and honestly. I am sure I asked him why he

was called Harris and what his father's name was but I have
forgotten what he said. "They told me in the store at Upper
Musquodoboit last fall that an Icelandic man called Harris
sometimes stopped there on his way from Dartmouth to
Truro. Was that you?"

"Yes," said Hafliđi. "I sometimes pass through Upper
Musquodoboit when I'm on my way to Truro. A lively fellow,
the shopkeeper there."

"He told me that you travel to Truro every fall," I said.

"I have gone there toward the end of the summer for the
past few years now," he said.

"He said also that you had told him that there was a little
boy in Truro who had asked you never to forget him."

"That is right."

"Is this an Icelandic boy?"

"Yes, Icelandic through and through."

"Is he related to you?"

"He was my son," said Hafliđi, "but he died. His grave is
in a little graveyard near Truro. I go there every year to care
for it."

"Where is your wife?" I asked.

"She died in Iceland," said Hafliđi, "and when she died I
left for America with my little Jón. He was eight years old. He
was not strong but he was a clever and lovable child. We
spent some time in Ontario and then we came to Nova
Scotia. I found work near Truro. Soon after that my boy took
sick and died. He said to me at the end, 'Please do not forget
me, Pabbi.'"

I moved from Nova Scotia to Winnipeg in June of 1882.
At that time, Hafliđi was working at Cameron's sawmill. I
went there to say goodbye to him. I asked him whether he

would be moving to the Red River Valley soon. He thought that would not happen. More than likely, he would settle near Truro. I have never heard from him since.

THE PEDLAR

A few strangers made their way through the Icelandic settlement in Mooseland Hills during the years 1875 to 1882; missionaries, newspaper reporters, prospectors and hunters. None of them stayed for any length of time or received much attention as far as I can recall, with perhaps one exception. He was a pedlar who visited us and the Scottish neighbours to the east of us in the fall of 1881. He was unforgettable, and I have always been grateful to him for reasons that I will explain later.

He had come on foot from the ocean to the east of us and he only travelled short distances each day. He carried two large cases, one on his back and the other in front. Those cases contained small wares of many kinds; needles, thread, thimbles, clasps, buttons and so forth. He was a tall man, fairly lean and dark-haired, and he had a scraggly beard on his cheeks and his chin. He had a long hooked nose and small, coal-black eyes, rather hard and sharp-looking. He said his name was Aron Hassam and he said that he was Syrian, and that he had been born and raised in Hamburg, Germany. (Some thought he had called himself Abu Hassam.) He could speak Danish because he used that language to chat with one of the older men in our group, and he spoke German to an Austrian man who lived in the mining town of Tangier. English-speaking people said that he spoke good English, although he had an unusual accent.

When he came to Mooseland Hills, some of the Icelanders had already left because departures from the settlement began in the summer of 1881. At that time he was not likely to make many sales, but he stopped at every house that was still occupied as he travelled along the road. As soon as he stepped over the threshold he would say, "My name is Aron Hassam. I am a pedlar and I sell good wares at low prices." What he said was true because all his goods were offered at unusually low prices.

Some people said to him, "We cannot buy anything because we have no money." Then he said, "I can wait for my pay until Christmastime." Then people often said, "We can probably never pay you." Then he smiled and said, "That does not matter. I will lend to you anyway." We thought that this was very strange. In the end there were usually small purchases made but they were always paid for right away. When he was leaving each home he always asked the name of the farmer in the next house. In this way he was able to greet each man by name when he arrived.

I remember very well when this unusual travelling salesman came to my parents' home. It was around noon on a Saturday. He walked slowly up the hill to where our house stood and from a distance he looked rather queer. He wore a long, dark cloak, he had a black, broad-brimmed hat on his head and he carried a short stick in his right hand. When he had actually come into the house and set his bags down we felt better about him. My mother bought a thimble, a spool of white thread and a few needles. Then he asked her for a drink of water. She gave him some milk and he was obviously glad to get that. He sipped the milk slowly while he studied a landscape picture that we had on the wall. When he had finished all that was in the bowl he set it on the table, bowed to my mother and said, "I thank you for the milk. It was good. Syrian pedlars are not often treated with such hospitality, except among Icelanders." When he was leaving he asked me the name of the farmer in the next house to the east. I told him that.

"What are you saying?"

He looked at me sharply. "That is not an Icelandic name."

"No, he is Scottish," I said.

"Wasn't there an Icelandic farmer there before?" he asked.

"Yes," I said, "but he sold his land and left this summer to go to the Red River Valley."

"We will all go there," said the pedlar. With that he said goodbye to my mother and me and he left us.

That day he only went as far as the next house. He asked whether he might stay there until Monday morning because he said that it was not his custom to travel on Sundays. He was told that he would be welcome to stay.

As it happened, on Sunday I went with another Icelandic boy about my age over to the neighbour's house. There sat the pedlar on the steps outside the house. He was reading from a small book with a beautiful cover. We greeted him and he responded cheerfully. He asked our names, our ages, how far we were in our school grades. He wanted to know whether we could read Icelandic as well as English. He seemed pleased when we told him that we could read Icelandic fairly well, likely better than English. Then we asked him what he was reading.

"I am reading the Talmud," he said, "or, rather, an abstract of the Talmud. It is written in a language that you cannot understand. In this book there are many good rules. The Talmud tells people how they should live. Not everyone knows the art of living well."

We boys asked him to tell us some rules from the Talmud.

"Here is a good one," he said. "Teach your tongue to say 'I do not know.' Here is another good one. Your friend has a friend and your friend's friend has a friend. Be heedful what you say and careful how you act." He told us many other things but much of it was hard to understand. We did not find him unpleasant at all except perhaps his eyes, which were dark and sharp.

After a while the Scottish farmer came out of the house and started talking to the pedlar and asking him questions. One of the questions was whether he had ever met Icelandic people before this visit to the settlement.

"I met some Icelanders when I was in Copenhagen," said the pedlar, "and I went to Iceland in 1874 and I met several people there."

"What errand did you have in Iceland?" asked the Scot.

"I went with my brother."

"What was his business?"

"My brother had studied the Scandinavian languages. He had read a lot about Iceland and he very much wanted to see the country with his own eyes. And there were big celebrations in Iceland that summer."

The pedlar and the farmer discussed many things while my friend and I were there, but I have forgotten most of the details.

Aron Hassam spent three nights in the Mooseland Hills. The last night he spent in the home of the schoolteacher.

This house was in the middle of the settlement and he had passed the house twice without stopping. He had decided that he would not stop there until he was on the point of leaving our area. He was received particularly well in the schoolmaster's house and he was given a good bed. In the morning he rose early, had a quick breakfast and gave a few coins to each of the couple's two young children. Then he set off to the west and down into the Musquodoboit Valley. He never returned to the Icelandic settlement.

As has been mentioned before, the departure of Icelandic people from Nova Scotia began in the summer of 1881 and by the next summer all had left from the settlement. My mother, my sister and I were the last ones to leave, in late June of 1882. By that time I was almost sixteen years old and my sister was in her ninth year. Our destination was Winnipeg because my father had gone there the previous autumn. We were the only Icelandic people travelling at that time, with the exception of one young woman who had been working in a house in Halifax for a few years. When we reached the Great Lakes we boarded ship at Collingwood bound for Duluth, Minnesota, and from there we were to go by train to Winnipeg. Most of the settlers had taken the same route when they moved west.

On the way from Collingwood to Duluth something happened that was really not important, but I have never forgotten it; it is a story in itself. The ship left Collingwood late in the afternoon. The winds were calm, the sky was clear and a full moon arose. There were many passengers: English, Scottish, Irish and folks from eastern Canada. As the evening wore on, a few men gathered on the deck at the back of the ship. Some sat on benches, some leaned against the gunwale, and they talked about all kinds of things but especially about Winnipeg and the Red River Valley. In my mind I still carry a picture of those well-dressed, healthy-looking men who stood on the deck in the twilight that fine evening. Some of them were beardless young men, some had moustaches and looked to be in their in their thirties, and then there were a few middle-aged men with full beards. Some of them looked quite prosperous. There were no older men among them.

I do not know how it happened but all of a sudden I found myself in their midst and I started talking to a chap who had been laughing and carrying on a loud conversation. He looked to be about twenty-five years old; he was tall and slim, fair-skinned and quite handsome. He was full of energy and exuberance. Very quickly he found out that I was Icelandic. Then he started telling everyone that he had been in Manitoba the year before and that he had met some Icelanders while working on the railroad there. He told several stories about his dealings with them. All of the stories resembled the Icelandic folk tales about the comic characters, the brothers from Bakki (Eirik, Gisli and Helgi). Some of the listeners seemed to get a lot of fun out of this, and indeed the young man was a good storyteller. I realized right away that this chap was full of pranks and that he was trying to tease me by telling these ridiculous tales. Nevertheless, I was a little angry and I let him know that I was displeased. I went so far as to ask people not to listen to this balderdash. Of course I said some foolish things and therefore made things worse. The storyteller went on and on, and some of the men were practically bursting with laughter. I soon realized that it would be best for me to keep quiet, which I did, although it was difficult under the circumstances. Then suddenly I heard a deep voice.

"Young man, you have told the boy so many comical stories about Icelanders that now it is time to tell some other kinds of stories about them. I know a good one that I would be happy to tell you if you would kindly let me have a turn."

All the men looked toward the speaker. He sat beside the gunwale in the shadows. He looked to be quite a big man and well-dressed. I could not see his face very well because he wore a wide-brimmed hat but I thought I recognized that voice.

"Yes, by all means, tell us a good story about an Icelander," said several men from the group, including the joker. The deep-voiced man remained where he sat and proceeded to tell his story. He spoke clearly, slowly and quietly. All seemed to give him their full attention. This is his story.

In the summer of 1850 an Icelander travelled on a Danish ship to New York and for some reason he remained there. His name was Erik Holt (or Holtman). He was a big man, good-looking, with fair hair and blue eyes. He soon found a good job working for a Danish merchant in the city. He established himself, married a good woman of Swedish descent and built a pleasant house in the suburbs. He won many friends and everything was going according to his wishes. But all of a sudden he fell into debt and lost all his holdings. Few people knew how it had happened. He was left penniless with a wife and two young children by the time that the debt was cleared up. He had sold his house, the lot, the furniture and even his overcoat. He was determined to be free of that debt.

Soon after, he left to go to California to look for gold and he was lucky. He spent two years there, then he moved back east and started a grocery business in a fairly large city in Pennsylvania. He was well respected by people he met there and his company flourished. He built a good home, sent his children to good schools as they grew up, helped the poor, was careful about making loans and avoided any debts. "Men are good," he said, "but they could be better." That was his saying. He often had young men in his employ. If any of them was late for work in the morning he lost a little money from his pay; if any of them worked overtime in the evening he received a generous bonus.

One time two prominent men from the city came to see him to ask if he would like to take part in a gift that was to be presented to a millionaire in honour of some contribution that he had made to the community. Erik Holt was not enthusiastic but he gave a small donation. When the list of contributions was drawn up his donation was the smallest one.

Soon afterward two other men approached him and asked if he would take part in a drive to set up a fund in aid of the sick and the poor in the city. He said he would send some money into the fund the following day. When the list of givings was published in the newspaper it was noted that no one had given as much as Erik Holt.

And so time went on. Then one day a couple of years ago a middle-aged man, rather sickly looking and poorly dressed, came to Erik Holt's store and asked for him. This poor fellow was told that Mr. Holt was in his house because he was not feeling well.

"Please tell him that an old man has come to see him on urgent business," said the newcomer. One of the clerks went into the house but came back quickly to say that Mr. Holt would like to know the man's name and his errand. The visitor would neither give his name or his business. He asked the clerk to go once more and tell Mr. Holt that it was important that he come into the store and allow a tired old man to exchange a few words with him. "If Mr. Holt comes out here he will soon recognize me," he said.

Finally Mr. Holt agreed to come out to the store and when he saw the poor, tattered man he was obviously quite startled.

'Oh, you—here!" he said, as he stared at his guest.

"I had to come," said the old man.

"Welcome!" said Mr. Holt, as he offered his hand.

"Thank you," said the other, as they shook hands.

"You will stay with us for a week or more," said Mr. Holt.

"Thank God!" said the visitor, as Erik Holt led him into his house.

The next day Mr. Holt and his guest were seen walking in the garden and they were always talking to each other. None of the clerks knew what their relationship was, but they noticed that now the guest was dressed in clean clothes with a white collar and tie and new shoes. The next day he had a new cane and a watch in his pocket. As the days went on he looked younger and stronger.

Two weeks went by. Then one morning Erik Holt accompanied his guest to the railway station, bought him a ticket to New York, gave him a wallet with a few ten dollar bills and wished him farewell. The clerks at the store were aware of some of this. They asked Erik Holt who the visitor had been but he never gave his name. All that Mr. Holt's son told them was this.

"When my father was a young man living in New York he met this man and they became friends. This man did not know how to manage money and he fell into hopeless debt. When he was having his worst problems he asked my father if he would be his guarantor. My father agreed to help and he took out a loan with his house and furniture as collateral. Soon after that his friend ran off to Canada or Mexico and my father lost everything he owned. Now this man came to be reconciled with us. You saw how my father received him."

This is the story that the deep-voiced man told that evening on board ship. All the men listened attentively. When he finished the story the man stood up and walked slowly along the deck. I saw that he was none other than Aron Hassam, the pedlar who came to the settlement in the Mooseland Hills the previous summer. Now he was shaven and he did not wear his cloak. He was neatly dressed in a light grey suit. I was not sure whether he recognized me but I thought he was looking at me at times as he told his story. When he had left one of the men said, "Was there a moral to that story?"

"That's up to each one to decide," said the joker who had upset me that evening. That was all that was said about that subject. The men began to talk about Winnipeg and the Red River Valley.

The next day I wanted to try to speak to Aron Hassam but I was not able to do that. I saw him a few times at a distance—that was all. When the ship landed at Duluth I noticed that he was one of the first passengers to step on shore. That was the last time I saw him, but I have always had warm feelings towards him.

AN OLD SEA WOLF

This is the story of an Icelandic man who had the strength of giants. His name was Hrómundur Bórðarson (Thordarson) and he was born and raised in the East fjords of Iceland. He was nearly fifty years old when he set out for the New World in 1875 with his wife, who was in delicate health, and their six young children. They settled on the East Coast of Nova Scotia. Although I did not see him often, I remember him particularly well.

He was a tall man, but his height was balanced by his broad back and barrel chest. His neck was thick and he had extremely muscular arms and legs. In appearance he was certainly not handsome. His forehead was low and furrowed, his eyebrows so bushy they were almost scary, his jaw was long and strong and his nose was bent and sharp. However, his eyes were extraordinary. They were a striking blue and his gaze was unwaveringly direct. His hair was fair and slightly curly, and he had a light-coloured, rather unkempt beard. He was certainly not educated and not particularly wise but he was, nevertheless, clever and capable in many ways.

Hrómundur made his home on a rugged island that lies beyond Spry Bay. This island is called Sailor's Woe and it comprises approximately one hundred acres. On the west side there are low, sandy beaches, but on the east side there are high cliffs. The Atlantic Ocean rams into these cliffs and the sea is always rough. Many a ship has been wrecked on those cliffs or on the reefs beyond. On this craggy island, Hrómundur kept a cow and a few sheep. To make ends meet, he relied on fishing. He used a craft intended for two men but he rowed out alone. He hauled his catch to the market-place at Spry Bay. He was known in the village for his endurance and was well regarded there. In those parts were mainly Irishmen and Scots, a sturdy lot who were well acquainted with the sea. Among them were the brothers O'Hara, the O'Brians, the McIsaacs, the Reids and the renowned Donald Gaskell, one of the strongest men in Atlantic Canada in his day. Donald had noticed Hrómundur and had observed his habits.

"This old Icelander! There's a man, lads, there's a man," said Donald.

Now for the story, which became almost legendary in Nova Scotia around this time. One day, in the fall of 1882, Hrómundur's wife took sick. That same morning gale-force winds came in from the northeast. Gales like this are not uncommon off Nova Scotia, and ships have often been battered and wrecked.

As the day went on, the woman's condition worsened and the storm grew more intense. Evening came and the wild weather continued. Hrómundur realized that time was of the essence, and he would have to get the help of the young and capable Dr. Patrick who lived in the village of Spry Bay.

But the village was more than five miles away and it was impossible to set out at night. He hoped that morning would bring some relief from the storm. There was no sleep that night and, when dawn came, the weather was worse than ever. His wife was in serious condition. Three times Hrómundur walked down to the ocean front, and three times he returned to the shanty to look at his wife and the six young children who were huddled around her bed. The decision was hard: to go or to stay? If he stayed, his children would be motherless by nightfall. If he set out, he might well perish in the channel and the children would be helpless on the island.

There was no other way. He had to set out for land no matter what. He said goodbye to his family, pushed out the big boat and set out to row to Spry Bay through the churning water.

At Spry Bay, men stood near the shore and looked out over the channel. A long peninsula juts out into the bay and forms a good harbour there, so that the water is usually safe when the wind blows in from the northeast. Beyond the point the sea is usually rough, even on a calm day.

The villagers stood down by the shore, the brothers O'Hara, the O'Brians, the McIsaacs, the Reids and big old Donald Gaskell, all seasoned sailors. The weather was terrible. "What's that out in the channel?" asked somebody there.

"It's a boat," said Donald Gaskell.

"There must be quite the crew to set out on a day like this," said another.

"There is only one man on that boat," said Donald, "and he is the old Icelander because the boat is coming from the island."

"Then he must be off his head," said someone.

"No, he has not gone crazy," said Donald. "There must be some trouble there. No one sets out in these conditions in a small open boat unless someone's life is at stake." No one took his eyes off the boat. They saw that the man rowed steadily ahead and moved across the channel fairly quickly because the wind was behind him. As the craft neared the point, the swirling waters were at the very worst and, for a while, it was doubtful whether the boat would come through but, finally, it made its way into the shelter of the harbour. The men rushed out into the water and hauled the boat into land. They gathered around Hrómundur and shouted questions.

"What are you trying to do? What made you set out into the storm?"

"Dr. Patrick! Dr. Patrick!" called Hrómundur, as he jumped out of the boat.

"Dr. Patrick lives on the top of the hill," said one of the men. "What do you want with him? Who is sick?"

"Dr. Patrick! Dr. Patrick!" was all that Hrómundur would say. He pushed people aside and strode up the steep hill towards the doctor's house.

Dr. Patrick was in his little office. He was about thirty years old, rather a small man but well built, with a plain face and coal-black hair. He saw a huge man run up the hill and he guessed what must be wrong. A sense of dread overtook him. When Hrómundur reached the house, he knocked on the door and then hurled it open and rushed in. "Doctor," he said. "My wife is sick." Hrómundur spoke in broken English. He made the doctor understand that he should come to the island immediately, and that Hrómundur would pay what- ever he asked for his trouble.

"The weather is wild," said the doctor. "It is out of the question to try to cross the channel. I cannot go with you until things calm down a bit."

"But my wife is sick," said Hrómundur.

"To set out into the bay today would mean death," said the doctor, "but I will come with you as soon as the weather improves."

"You have to come," said Hrómundur.

"Not for all the money in the world would I go out in this weather," said Dr. Patrick. "Not for the king or the pope would I set out today."

"But the woman will die!" said Hrómundur. "And there are six small children."

"I have a wife and children, too," said Dr. Patrick. "I just can't throw my life away and leave them. I'll say it once more—I'm not going to sea today."

Hrómundur stared at the doctor. His face changed colour. His hands clenched and his muscles stiffened. He turned suddenly and left the house. He rushed down the hillside towards the boat. The townsmen moved out of his path as he approached. Donald Gaskell laid a hand on his shoulder.

"Stay put, you old sea wolf," he said. "Stay with us until she settles a bit. Ten men will take you and the doctor out in O'Hara's big boat. As it stands, only a big steamship would make it across."

The men who were gathered there were all in agreement. Hrómundur said nothing but proceeded to push the boat out, inch by inch. It seemed as if he were weighing in his mind whether he should stay or go.

"Listen to me," said Donald. "Stay with us. It was tough getting here but it will be twice as bad getting back."

Hrómundur said nothing but proceeded to push the boat slowly out. By this time, Dr. Patrick had joined the group. He shouted at Hrómundur over and over and bade him to be

sensible and wait. He said he would come with him as soon
as the wind let up a bit. Several others tried to persuade him.
Hrómundur said nothing. The boat was almost launched.
Hrómundur turned very slowly and looked at the men who
stood at the shore. He looked towards the island and he
thought about his family. He looked at the swirling water at
the point and at the waves in the channel. He looked like a
man who has to jump over a canyon as a matter of life or
death and has to measure with his eyes how long the jump
must be. He weighed the odds.

All of a sudden, he whirled around and pounced like a
panther toward Donald Gaskell. Just as suddenly, he
switched direction, slipped through the crowd, snatched Dr.
Patrick in his arms, jumped into the boat, pushed off and
rowed like a madman.

Everyone was stunned. They did not realize what was
happening until the boat was in the water. As they came to
their senses, they heard Dr. Patrick call for help. Men ran for
their boats, which had been hauled well up on to shore. By
the time they reached their boats, Hrómundur was about to
turn and head into the riptide at the end of the point.

"Now it is too late to follow them," said Donald Gaskell,
and he knew what he was talking about. "It will be their
death and death to any of us who try to rescue Dr. Patrick
now. The boat would upset if you tried anything of the sort,
and it is better to lose two lives than ten or twelve. That old
giant will get to the island because he knows the sea better
then we do. What a man! We'll leave it to him from now on."

It was obvious that what Donald said was right. There
was no chance of rescuing Dr. Patrick now. In fact, a rescue
attempt would only distract Hrómundur. All the binoculars

that were available in Spry Bay were put to use that day. It was a good thing that Mrs. Patrick and the children were not at home while all this was happening.

As far as Dr. Patrick was concerned, as soon as he sat up in the boat he realized that he could not jump out and reach the shore because he was no swimmer. In spite of himself, he called for help. He saw the men run for their boats and at first he thought he would be saved before Hrómundur left the harbour area. When Hrómundur reached the point and headed into the roughest water, Dr. Patrick said his prayers.

All of a sudden he realized that there was a lot of water in the boat. He grabbed a bucket and began to bail. He breathed a sigh of relief when they crossed the worst part, but then they were headed into the channel. The wind had slowed a little but the waves were still too much for such a small boat. Dr. Patrick bailed and bailed, and as he worked faster and faster, his courage grew. He worked furiously, inspired by Hrómundur who rowed like a maniac, wordlessly and without the slightest pause. The perspiration rolled down his face. He used all his strength on the oars, which bent under the pressure. The boat did not move much with each swing of the oars but still they moved in the right direction. So they continued. One rowed, the other bailed and, when they finally reached the shelter of the island, they had won the battle. When they landed, Dr. Patrick noticed that blood oozed from every nail on Hrómundur's fingers.

By the time they arrived at the shanty it was beginning to get dark, but Hrómundur's wife was still alive. Dr. Patrick went straight to work. By morning, she was out of danger and Hrómundur's children numbered seven.

By dawn, the weather had cleared. At about nine o'clock

in the morning, Hrómundur's boat landed once more at Spry Bay. According to the story that they tell in the village thereabouts, Dr. Patrick's hair turned white from the adventure, but Hrómundur was his old self—silent, old-fashioned and tough. It was obvious that he was very fond of Dr. Patrick, and Dr. Patrick held no grudge against Hrómundur.

It was Donald Gaskell who suggested that folks get together and build a log house in the village for Hrómundur and his family. This they did, and they bought a few acres of land as well. All agreed that the island was no place for a couple with young children. Within a few weeks, the family had moved from the island to Spry Bay. Hrómundur lived out his life in the village. His children all received a good education, and one of his daughters married Dr. Patrick's eldest son.

It was Donald Gaskell who often told the story of someone from "away" who snatched a grown man out of the hands of a crowd of Scots and Irishmen and ran off with him in broad daylight. "That was a man," said Donald. "That was a man."

THE ICELANDIC
SHERLOCK HOLMES

Whenever I read A. Conan Doyle's stories of Sherlock Holmes I think of a certain Icelander whom I met in my younger days in Nova Scotia. When I met him he was in his early twenties, and if I remember correctly his name was Hallur Thorsteinsson. I know that he grew up in Iceland but I am not sure of the district where he lived, but I guess that he was from the East fjords because twice he sent letters to a woman who lived at Djúpavogi.

I always think of him when I read Sherlock Holmes because he is the only Icelander I have known who was gifted with all the qualities of a master spy or detective. If he had had a good education and the opportunity to put his talents into practice, I believe he would have become a celebrity in that line. I want to give you an account of some of the happenings which made me feel this way, but I want to begin by giving a short description of Hallur himself.

He did not resemble Sherlock Holmes in features or in build. In appearance, he was unremarkable. Certainly he did not look the part of a character from a detective story, either sleuth or criminal. Hallur was in fact a very small man, rather homely and harmless-looking. His eyes were intelligent and rather kindly, but they were small and usually looked half

closed, as if his eyelids were heavy. His head was propor-
tionately large, his face long and narrow and his posture
made him look rather downcast. His movements were slow
and he was usually quiet and withdrawn. In spite of his quiet
manner he was obviously curious by nature. He seldom
asked questions but it seemed that without any effort, he
uncovered men's secrets and became aware of things that
they were trying to hide. Like Lord Macaulay, he had an
unusually accurate memory and he never forgot a face.
Whenever he attended a gathering he remained on the outside, as it were, unnoticed. He always seemed to be off in a
corner, wherever he was, but still it was obvious that he was
very observant and took note of everything that went on
around him. He enjoyed chess and that seemed to be his
only recreation. He was considered to be a good player. He
was good at figures, although he had had very little formal
education, and he enjoyed riddles. He seemed rather unemo-
tional; neither overjoyed over good news nor visibly affected
by the sorrows of others. However, he never took advantage
of anyone and bore ill will to no one.

Hallur did not spend much time with Icelanders after he
came to America. To begin with at least he usually found
work with Canadian farmers, often for low wages. Many felt
that he was rather peculiar, but most people felt kindly
towards him and rather enjoyed his brusque comments.

One time, I recall, there was a notice in the paper to the
effect that a certain society lady from Halifax had lost a dia-
mond brooch at a masquerade party.

"The young widower must have stolen the brooch," said
Hallur to his friends. They had a good laugh over that and
most thought it was nonsense. Two years later, the same

fellows were stunned when the news came out that a young widower had been convicted of stealing the brooch. How Hallur came to know this or whether it was just an idle guess, no one could say, but they thought it rather remarkable.

One time a stranger came to the home where Hallur was staying. He wanted a drink and he asked for directions to the next town.

"Who was that fellow?" someone asked, after the stranger had left.

"He is an escaped prisoner and he used to be a book-keeper," said Hallur.

"How do you know that?" asked his friends.

"I can see in his eyes that he is running away but by look-ing at his right hand I can tell that he has been a bookkeeper," said Hallur. His companions took little note of these remarks until a few days later when it turned out that Hallur had come to correct conclusions.

One time I remember that Hallur visited the Icelandic set-tlement at Mooseland Hills. He came in the fall and spent a few days at the home where I was working. All the fellows thought he was most interesting. Three of us walked with him down to the main road, which led through the settle-ment. We noticed that someone had travelled along the way that morning, for there were recent wheel marks in the road. My companions and I guessed that a certain man we knew had driven his wagon eastward to the sea that morning.

"These marks were made by a two-wheeled cart that came from the east," argued Hallur, "and a man has pulled the cart, rather than a four-footed animal."

We checked the marks more closely and decided that

Hallur was likely right, because we could see no marks made by an ox or a horse but we could see footprints left by a man.

"Who could this have been?" we all wondered.

"Likely a pedlar," said Hallur. Here he did make a mistake, though. To be sure, we heard later that day that a man had travelled that way during the morning and he had pulled a two-wheeled cart. However, he was not a peddler, but a young prospector travelling from Tangier to the Moose River Mines. Although Hallur was not completely right in this instance, we were still impressed with his powers of observation.

But now I would like to tell you the story I found most interesting of all.

During the fall and winter of 1882-83, Hallur was working for a Scottish farmer near the railway centre at Shubenacadie, about forty miles from Halifax. At the same time there was a young man of Jewish descent who operated a small shop in the village there. I never heard his full name but the townspeople called him Joe. His store was on the main street of the town and he dealt in small housewares, novelties and used clothing. He had started his business with practically no funds and he was anxious to succeed. He was hard-working and reliable and had earned a good reputation in the community. Business had been good during the summer of 1882 and he had set aside one hundred dollars, which he intended to put into a savings account in Halifax when he went there to do some buying in the fall. The night before he planned to go to the city, the money disappeared from a locked safe in the store. The most remarkable thing was that nothing disappeared from the safe or from the store except for those one hundred dollars. Yet there were many valuable items in the store and in the safe were one hundred and fifty dollars besides the hundred dollars, which had been set aside for savings. Strangely enough there was no evidence of anyone having broken into the store. Doors, windows and the safe were just as the shopkeeper had left them the night before—all locked, unbroken and nothing disturbed—except the one hundred dollars.

The house where Joe lived was rather small with a flat roof. There was the store and, to one side, there was the kitchen and a small sitting room. From the sitting room there were stairs leading to the two small rooms on the upper level. The young man slept in one room and his mother and his ten-year-old sister slept in the other. These three were the only people who lived in the house. On the storefront there was one big window that faced the main street and it could only be opened from the inside. The thief had not gone in that window, and there was no evidence that he had even tried it. There were two doors to the store; first, a main door out to the street and, secondly, a door from the store into the sitting room. The front door had a good lock and was also bolted from within. The other door into the sitting room admittedly could be unlocked with a skeleton key. Then there was the back door to the kitchen. That door was not very secure, and the kitchen window and the sitting-room window could easily be opened from the outside and entry gained that way.

It was decided that the likeliest explanation was that the thief had come in the back door to the kitchen, opened the inside door to the store with a skeleton key and figured out how to open and lock the safe, because there was no key to it. This was the best explanation that was brought forward.

But no one could explain why the thief would take exactly the sum that was set aside for savings and did not touch anything else, either money or other valuables.

A great deal of effort was put forth to try to find the thief, but all to no avail. The poor young shopkeeper was grieved over the loss of such a sum of money, but still he was as pleasant as usual. He moved the safe into his bedroom, reinforced the window, put a good lock on the door and made a habit of locking it every night before he got ready for bed. He also kept a loaded pistol at hand to make sure that no money would be taken from his safe again.

Soon it was Christmastime.

Joe, the shopkeeper, did a good business—even better than before—and by New Year's he had gained enough to set aside another one hundred dollars. He wanted to get these into a bank as soon as possible. He decided that he would travel to Halifax on the first Monday in January. The evening before, about ten o'clock, he counted out his money. He had three hundred and ten dollars and some cents. He put the money in his wallet, laid the wallet in the safe, locked it as usual and then got ready for bed and went to sleep. In the morning when he got up and opened the safe, there were two hundred and ten dollars and a few cents in his wallet. One hundred dollars had disappeared during the night while he slept, and they were exactly the bills that he had intended to take to the bank. He had put a blue string around a bunch of bills and had put them in a special compartment in his wallet. The poor young shopkeeper was both grieved and angry and simply could not understand how the money could have disappeared. He wondered about some form of witchcraft. The door to his bedroom was locked with the key in it on the inside, the window did not look as if it had been tampered with at all and on the lower floor there was no evidence that anyone had forced himself in either through the doors or the windows. During the night there had been new snow, so there would have been noticeable tracks if there had been anyone around the house during the latter part of the night. But there were no tracks to be seen.

This was clearly a most peculiar happening and it led to a great deal of speculation in the community when the news got out. Some people thought that Joe was making this up or that he had counted his money incorrectly or that he was crazy. Others thought that the old woman, his mother, had fooled him both times, had taken the two hundred dollars and meant to keep them at home in case of emergency. Some reckoned that the old woman did not want her son to put his money in the bank, because she had heard of banks going broke.

A detective came from Halifax to investigate the matter. Some said he was not very experienced but he tried everything that he could think of and followed all the tricks of the trade. He measured the house from top to bottom, studied every nook and cranny and every board, and finally came to the conclusion that the thief had gotten up on the roof on the Sunday evening, just when it started to snow, and had climbed down the chimney, which was unusually roomy, and had gotten into the shopkeeper's bedroom that way. Then he had gotten out of the house before it stopped snowing, and therefore left no tracks in the morning.

This story did not seem likely, but it was felt that it was not impossible that a thief had gotten into the bedroom through the fireplace. The chimney had not been taken into consideration before. But the question still remained—why did the thief not take all the money in the safe, since it was money that he was after? Why did he not take the wallet, with all its contents? Why did he go to the trouble of locking the safe before he left? It took a little time to do so and most burglars do not stand around any longer than necessary when they are stealing. This certainly must have been an unusual thief. In fact, he was unlike all other thieves. He must belong to a new class of burglar altogether—more cunning, more courageous, more courteous and more considerate than burglars usually are. He did not startle anyone, he did not take everything valuable that his victim had, he damaged nothing and he left everything as it was, and he went with only one-third of the money. What a strange criminal! What a thief!

Everyone in the community talked about this but no one could bring up a satisfactory solution. The thief was nowhere to be found and there seemed to be no way of catching him. The detective went back to Halifax. Joe offered a reward of one hundred dollars to anyone who could find the thief.

At this point, Hallur enters the story. He had been considering this case and turning it over in his mind. He felt that this was like a riddle or a problem in arithmetic or a game of chess—how did the money disappear and who was the thief? He mentioned to his employer that he thought he could find the thief and probably the money as well.

His employer went and spoke to the shopkeeper and told him that he knew of a man who might be able to point out the thief who had taken his money. Of course the shopkeeper was very excited. He asked Mr. Miller, Hallur's employer, to come with him across the street to discuss this matter in front of the judge, a man named Seller.

They walked over to the judge's office and Joe immediately said that Mr. Miller knew a man who could point to the thief. He wanted the judge to talk to the man on his behalf.

"Who is this man?" asked Judge Seller.

"He is just my hired man. He is a young fellow and an Icelander at that."

"A young fellow and an Icelander at that!" said Seller, and made a face. "He must be a sly one if he can solve the type of riddle that a trained detective gives up on. Of course they eat a lot of fish in Iceland so they likely have good brains. But does this foreigner really expect to be able to find the thief?"

"He is sure he can do it," said Miller, "and he will likely find the money, too. I trust he will receive the hundred-dollar reward without any problem."

"I shall live up to my promise as far as that is concerned," said Joe.

Judge Seller said that they should proceed with caution and not count on this too much. He said that he did not put much faith in common labourers as far as such matters were concerned, especially foreigners. He said that in similar circumstances he had known of greedy and uneducated labourers who accused innocent people of stealing and other crimes in the hopes of claiming a reward. Of course, he said it was possible that Hallur was an honest and a clever man, but he certainly had not been convinced of that.

They chatted back and forth for a while and then decided that they would all meet the next day in Joe's shop, and there they would hear what evidence Hallur could bring forth to prove his theory.

The next day, according to plan, they all gathered at the shop. Hallur asked to be allowed to check the bedroom where the shopkeeper slept, so they all went upstairs. Hallur quickly checked the lock on the door, looked at the safe, gave the fireplace a glance out of the corner of his eye, looked around the room and then seemed to study the bed with the greatest attention.

"Well, my friend," said Judge Seller, "can you name the thief and locate the money for us?"

"I can point out the thief," said Hallur, innocently, "and I can guess where the money is."

"Tell us who the thief is," said Seller. "We can look for the money, if it has not been spent, after we have taken the thief into custody."

"But I would not like to see the thief taken prisoner," said Hallur seriously. "I would like to see him forgiven."

A strange expression came over the judge's face and he looked dubiously at Hallur.

"No letting him off," he said. "We'll have to take him prisoner if we can find him."

"Is that absolutely necessary?" asked Hallur sadly.

"Yes, definitely," said the judge. "We'll make no exceptions! Who is the thief?"

"If the shopkeeper gives his permission, I will point him out to you," said Hallur. Joe gave his permission.

Hallur looked at the judge in silence for a moment, then slowly moved towards the shopkeeper, slapped him on the shoulder and said, "You, sir, are the thief!"

The shopkeeper was amazed. Mr. Miller was stunned, and the judge was so taken aback that he moved towards the door as if he was getting ready to take his leave. He felt sure that Hallur was crazy. There was complete silence in the room for a moment.

"I?" said Joe. "Am I the thief?"

"Yes," said Hallur.

"My dear friend, what are you saying?" asked Mr. Miller, trying hard to swallow.

"The man is crazy," said the judge. "I always expected that but now I know it for sure."

"Allow me to explain," said Hallur, slowly and calmly. "The shopkeeper is a thief without knowing it himself. He has stolen from himself while he was sleeping. He has walked in his sleep. While awake and asleep, he has been thinking about the money he wanted to put in the bank. He dreamed that he was in Halifax, dreamed that he was in the bank. In his sleep he got up, opened the safe, took the right amount out of his wallet, locked the safe and hid the money."

At this point, the shopkeeper's mother came into the room. She had heard what Hallur had said.

"This could well be," she said, "because my son had a habit of sleepwalking when he was a boy, although I have not been aware of his doing that recently."

"But where did he hide the money?" asked the judge, and started to move back into the room.

"In the mattress, of course," said Hallur, "since the safe is the only cupboard in the room. In his sleep he thought that the mattress was the bank."

Joe and the judge rushed up to the bed and lifted up the mattress. In one corner of the mattress cover there was a little opening. Joe put his hand in there and pulled it out quickly. He had found all the money—two hundred dollars! All stared in amazement—except Hallur.

Joe immediately gave Hallur half the money he had found in the mattress and said that he hoped that as little as possible would be said about this matter.

When Hallur came down the stairs, he heard Judge Seller mutter to himself, "This Icelander must be the devil himself!"

Hallur stayed in Shubenacadie for the rest of the winter but in the spring he went to Halifax and from there, a short time later, he moved to Boston. Since then, I have not heard from him. But I always think of him when I read the adventures of Sherlock Holmes.